CCNP Cisco Networking Academy Program:
Semester Five Lab Companion
Advanced Routing

Cisco Systems, Inc.

Cisco Networking Academy Program

Mark McGregor

Cisco Press

Cisco Press
201 West 103rd Street
Indianapolis, IN 46290 USA

CCNP Cisco Networking Academy Program:
Semester Five Lab Companion
Advanced Routing

Cisco Systems, Inc.

Cisco Networking Academy Program

Mark McGregor

Cisco Press logo is a trademark of Cisco Systems, Inc.

Published by:
Cisco Press
210 West 103rd Street
Indianapolis, IN 46290 USA

Printed in the United States of America   1 2 3 4 5 6 7 8 9 0

ISBN: 1-57870-234-8

Warning and Disclaimer

This book is designed to provide information on networking fundamentals. Every effort has been made to make this book as complete and as accurate as possible, but no warranty or fitness is implied.

The information is provided on an as-is basis. The author, Cisco Press, and Cisco Systems, Inc., shall have neither liability nor responsibility to any person or entity with respect to any loss or damages arising from the information contained in this book or from the use of the programs that may accompany it.

The opinions expressed in this book belong to the author and are not necessarily those of Cisco Systems, Inc.

Trademark Acknowledgments

All terms mentioned in this book that are known to be trademarks or service marks have been appropriately capitalized. Cisco Press or Cisco Systems, Inc., cannot attest to the accuracy of this information. Use of a term in this book should not be regarded as affecting the validity of any trademark or service mark.

Feedback Information

At Cisco Press, our goal is to create in-depth technical books of the highest quality and value. Each book is crafted with care and precision, undergoing rigorous development that involves the unique expertise of members of the professional technical community.

Readers' feedback is a natural continuation of this process. If you have any comments regarding how we could improve the quality of this book, or otherwise alter it to better suit your needs, you can contact us at feedback@ciscopress.com. Please be sure to include the book title and ISBN in your message.

We greatly appreciate your assistance.

Publisher	John Wait
Executive Editor	Carl Lindholm
Cisco Systems Program Manager	Bob Anstey
Product Manager	Shannon Gross
Managing Editor	Patrick Kanouse
Senior Project Editor	Sheri Replin
Copy Editor	Gayle Johnson

About the Author

Mark McGregor, CCNP, CCDP, CCAI, is the regional coordinator for the Cisco Networking Academy Program at Los Medanos College in Pittsburg, California. He has taught in the Networking Academy program since 1997, and currently works for Cisco Systems Worldwide Education. McGregor holds a bachelor's degree in English from the University of California, Davis and has been an author and contributor for Cisco Press since 1998. As a public school instructor for more than seven years, he has enjoyed the opportunity to teach and learn from students of all ages and backgrounds. He lives in Antioch, California.

Acknowledgments

The labs and activities in this manual were developed and tested by a talented team of experts, teachers, and students. Much of the material included in this manual was contributed by my teammates at Cisco Worldwide Education: Scott T. Wolfe, Bob Larson, Jim Yoshida, and Torrey Suzuki. This book is a direct product of their diligence, inventiveness, and expertise.

Wayne Lewis, my partner at Cisco WWE, deserves special thanks for keeping this project on track and for keeping me sane.

I am forever indebted to the fantastic team at Cisco Press, whose unenviable task has been to work with me in a deadline-oriented environment. This book owes its existence to the outstanding work of Carl Lindholm, Sheri Replin, Patrick Kanouse, and Gayle Johnson. Also, I must also single out Shannon Gross for taking such great care of me.

Finally, I thank my friend, Eric Yu, for the significant technical contributions he made to this book.

Table of Contents

Introduction

This manual provides a collection of lab exercises designed to supplement your study of advanced routing concepts and the Cisco IOS. The concepts covered in these exercises include advanced IP addressing techniques, DHCP, IP helper addresses, dynamic routing, static routing, default routing, single-area OSPF, point-to-multipoint OSPF, multiarea OSPF, EIGRP, route summarization, route redistribution, route filters, route maps, policy routing, BGP, and network security.

The labs are specifically written to supplement the Advanced Routing (Semester 5) course of the Cisco Networking Academy Program, but they can be used by anyone seeking hands-on experience and CCNP certification. Although the lab exercises contain brief explanations of key concepts, this manual is not a textbook. You will get the most out of these activities if you do them while concurrently engaged in formal study, such as an Advanced Routing Networking Academy class, a Building Cisco Scalable Networks class (offered by Cisco's Worldwide Training partners), or self-study using one of the following Cisco Press books:

- *CCNP Cisco Networking Academy Program: Semester Five Companion Guide, Advanced Routing* (ISBN: 1-58713-011-4)

- *Building Scalable Cisco Networks* (ISBN: 1-57870-228-3)

This lab manual includes a description of the lab configuration required to perform the exercises, a business scenario and WAN topology, an introductory lab, 10 groups of lab exercises, 4 challenge labs, and a command-reference appendix.

Each lab references the fictitious International Travel Agency (ITA), which maintains a global data network. The ITA business scenario provides a tangible, real-world application for each of the concepts introduced in the labs. A diagram of ITA's WAN topology is included in this lab manual so that students can familiarize themselves with the company and its network.

An introductory lab precedes the lab exercises and is intended to refresh your basic router configuration skills. Students who have just completed their CCNA studies can use this activity to better acquaint themselves with the lab environment. The introductory lab should be completed before beginning the lab exercises.

The lab exercises introduce you to advanced IOS configuration commands in a structured activity. They are grouped according to topic, corresponding to the chapters in *CCNP Cisco Networking Academy Program: Semester Five Companion Guide, Advanced Routing*. Each exercise group contains two to four labs:

- Chapter 1: An Overview of Scalable Networks
- Chapter 2: IP Addressing
- Chapter 3: Routing Overview
- Chapter 4: OSPF in a Single Area
- Chapter 5: Multiarea OSPF
- Chapter 6: EIGRP
- Chapter 7: Route Optimization
- Chapter 8: BGP
- Chapter 9: Scaling BGP
- Chapter 10: Security

If the concepts presented here are new to you, you should work through the exercises sequentially. After you are familiar with the concepts and essential IOS commands, you can focus your studies on particular exercises or challenge labs.

The challenge labs are an opportunity for you to apply the configuration concepts and commands introduced in the lab exercises. There are four challenge labs:

- OSPF
- EIGRP
- Route Optimization
- BGP

You can use these as a culminating activity, a timed test, or a group project.

Finally, this manual concludes with a command summary; you can use this as a quick reference or as a study guide.

Lab Equipment Requirements

CCNP Networking Academies

Each lab in this manual is written to accommodate the CCNP Academy lab pack, which CCNP Cisco Networking Academies are required to maintain. If your site has this lab pack, you can create up to three separate lab pods, using 2621 series routers as the middle router. Each pod requires no more than three routers and one switch (or hub), although Challenge Labs might require you to interconnect two pods.

Lab 4-3 requires the use of a Frame Relay switch. CCNP Academy lab packs contain at least one Adtran Atlas 550, which can be used as a Frame Relay switch. We recommend that each pod be equipped with an Atlas 550. The appropriate Atlas 550 configuration file is available to authorized Networking Academy instructors at cisco.netacad.net.

Alternatively, a Cisco router with at least three serial interfaces can be configured as a Frame Relay switch. Lab 4-3 includes a sample Frame Relay configuration for this purpose.

Three workstations with terminal programs, Ethernet NICs, TCP/IP software, and a Web browser are also required in each pod. This manual assumes that you are using Microsoft Windows as your workstation's operating system.

Independent Lab Environments

If you do not have access to the CCNP Academy lab pack, you can build your own pod with the appropriate Cisco routers. We recommend two 2620 series routers (a single Fast Ethernet interface) and one 2621 router (dual Fast Ethernet interfaces). In addition, you will need three pairs of DTE/DCE cables appropriate to the serial interfaces on the routers you are using.

Other Considerations

These lab exercises were written and tested using Cisco IOS release 12.0(5)T. Although this release is not required to run these labs, note that features and command syntax change with each IOS release.

A physical diagram containing the essential configuration information precedes each exercise. Because the labs can be performed on a variety of equipment, the interface numbering labeled in the lab diagrams may not match your specific devices. Command output, when included in the labs, reflects what students see if they use the standard CCNP Academy lab pack.

Case Study: International Travel Agency

International Travel Agency

International Travel Agency, Inc. creates unique excursions throughout the world. Its innovative adventures include Saharan safaris, European museum tours, and Great Barrier Reef charters. Regional offices allow travel agents to personally coordinate every detail and guarantee customer satisfaction.

Based in San Jose, International Travel Agency maintains a comprehensive database of travel adventure packages. Graphic artists provide an interactive, media-rich Web site with "virtual excursions," tempting potential clients. Also, in partnership with every major airline, cruise line, and resort, ITA is a leader in the use of extranets to cross-reference databases, allowing real-time updates for accurate reservations.

As a network professional with International Travel Agency, your responsibilities include creating and maintaining the San Jose campus network, connectivity to all regional headquarters, and Internet access via one or more service providers.

Company Structure and Locations

Corporate headquarters: San Jose, California, USA

- North American headquarters: San Jose, California, USA
  - East Tasman site
  - West Tasman site
  - Baypointe site
  - Vista, Montana site
- Asian headquarters: Singapore, Singapore
- Pacific headquarters: Auckland, New Zealand
- European headquarters: London, England
- African headquarters: Cape Town, South Africa

Router Names

ITA North America	ITA International	Service Providers
SanJose1	Singapore	ISP1A
SanJose2	Auckland	ISP1B
SanJose3	London	ISP2
Eastasman	Capetown	
Westasman		
Baypointe		
Vista		

The International Travel Agency (ITA) WAN Topology

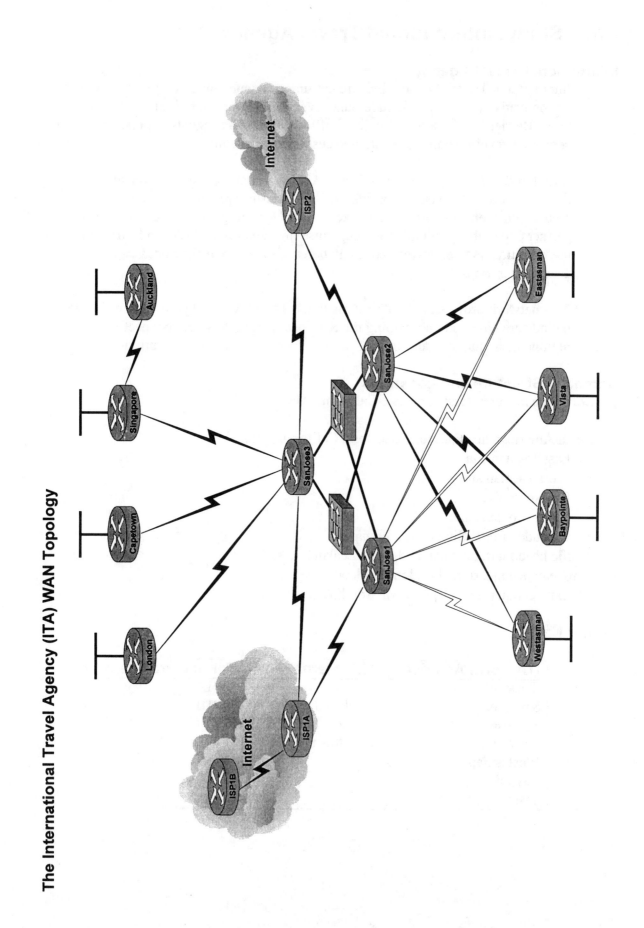

Introductory Lab 1: Getting Started and Building Start.TXT

Objective

This lab introduces the CCNP lab equipment and some IOS features that might be new to you. This introductory activity also describes how to use a simple text editor to create all (or part) of a router configuration file. After you create a text configuration file, you can apply that configuration to a router quickly and easily by using the techniques described in this lab.

Equipment Requirements

- A single router, preferably a 2600 series router, and a workstation running a Windows operating system
- One 3 1/2-inch floppy disk with label

Preliminary

Modular interfaces. Cisco routers can come with a variety of interface configurations. Some models have only fixed interfaces, meaning that the interfaces can't be changed or replaced by the user. Other models have one or more modular interfaces, allowing the user to add, remove, or replace interfaces as needed.

You might already be familiar with fixed interface identification, such as Serial 0, S0, Ethernet 0, and E0. Modular routers use notation such as Serial 0/0 or S0/1, where the first number refers to the module and the second number refers to the interface. Both notations use 0 as their starting reference, so S0/1 indicates that there is another serial interface S0/0.

Fast Ethernet. Many routers today are equipped with Fast Ethernet (10/100 Mbps autosensing) interfaces. You must use Fast Ethernet 0/0 or Fa0/0 on routers with Fast Ethernet interfaces.

The ip subnet-zero command. The **ip subnet-zero** command is enabled by default in IOS 12. This command allows you to assign IP addresses in the first subnet, called subnet 0. Because subnet 0 uses only binary zeros in the subnet field, its subnet address can potentially be confused with the major network address. With the advent of classless IP, the use of subnet 0 has become more and more common. The labs in this manual assume that you can assign addresses to the router's interfaces using subnet 0. If you are using any routers that have an IOS earlier than 12.0, you must add the global configuration command, **ip subnet-zero**, to your router's configuration.

No shutdown. Interfaces are shut down by default. Remember to explicitly issue a **no shutdown** command in interface configuration mode when you are ready to bring up the interface.

Passwords. The login command is applied to virtual terminals by default. This means that in order for your router to accept Telnet connections, you must configure a password. Otherwise, your router will not allow a Telnet connection, replying with the error message "password required, but none set."

Step 1

Take a few moments to examine your router. Familiarize yourself with any serial, BRI (ISDN), PRI (ISDN), and DSU/CSU interfaces on the router. Pay particular attention to any connectors or cables that are new to you.

Step 2

Establish a HyperTerminal session to the router.

Enter privileged EXEC mode.

Step 3

To clear the configuration, issue the erase start command.

Confirm your intentions when prompted, and answer "no" if you're asked to save changes. The result should look something like this:

```
Router#erase start
Erasing the nvram filesystem will remove all files! Continue?
[confirm]
[OK]
Erase of nvram: complete
Router#
```

When the prompt returns, issue the reload command.

Confirm your intentions when prompted. After the router finishes the boot process, choose not to use the AutoInstall feature, as shown:

```
Would you like to enter the initial configuration dialog? [yes/no]:
    no
Would you like to terminate autoinstall? [yes]: ← Press Enter to
    accept default.
Press RETURN to get started!
```

Step 4

In privileged mode, enter the show run command.

Note the following default configurations as you scroll through the running configuration:

- The version number of the IOS
- The ip subnet-zero command, which allows you to use subnet 0

- Each available interface and its name (*Note:* Each interface has the **shutdown** command applied to its configuration.)
- The **no ip http server** command, which prevents the router from being accessed by a Web browser
- No passwords are set for CON, AUX, and VTY sessions, as shown here:

```
line con 0
 transport input none
line aux 0
line vty 0 4
```

Using Copy and Paste with Notepad

In the next steps, you use the copy and paste feature to edit router configurations. You need to create a text file that can be pasted into your labs and used as a starting point for your router configuration. Specifically, you must build a login configuration that you can use with every lab included in this manual.

Step 5

If necessary, issue the **show run** command again so that **line con** and **line vty** are showing on your screen:

```
no ip http server
!
!
line con 0
 transport input none
line aux 0
line vty 0 4
!
end
```

Select the text as shown above and choose the Copy command from HyperTerminal's Edit menu.

Next, open Notepad, which is typically found on the Start menu under Programs, Accessories. After Notepad opens, select Paste from the Notepad Edit menu.

Edit the lines in Notepad to look like the following lines (the one-space indent is optional):

```
enable secret class
line con 0
 password cisco
 login
line aux 0
 password cisco
 login
line vty 0 4
 password cisco
 login
```

This configuration sets the enable secret to **class** and requires a login for all console, AUX port (usually a modem), and virtual terminal (Telnet) connections. The password for these connections is set to **cisco**. *Note:* Each of the passwords can be set to something else if you desire.

Step 6

Save the open file in Notepad to a floppy disk as **start.txt**.

Select all the lines in your Notepad document and choose Edit, Copy.

Step 7

Use the Windows taskbar to return to your HyperTerminal session, and enter global configuration mode.

From HyperTerminal's Edit menu, choose Paste to Host.

Issue the **show run** command to see if your configuration looks okay.

As a shortcut, you can now paste the contents of your **start.txt** file to any router before getting started with a lab.

Other Useful Commands

To enhance your **start.txt** file, you might consider adding one of the following commands:

- **ip subnet-zero** ensures that an older IOS allows IP addresses from subnet 0.
- **ip http server** allows you to access your routers using a Web browser. Although this configuration might not be desirable on a production router, it does give you an HTTP server for testing purposes in the lab.
- **no ip domain-lookup** prevents the router from attempting to query a DNS when you input a word that is not recognized as a command or a host table entry. This saves you time if you make a typo or misspell a command.
- **logging synchronous** in the **line con 0** configuration returns you to a fresh line when your input is interrupted by a console logging message.
- **configure terminal (conf f)** can be used in your file so that you don't have to type that command before pasting the contents of the file to the router.

Step 8

Use the Windows taskbar to return to Notepad and edit the lines so that they read as shown:

```
config t
!
enable secret class
ip subnet-zero
ip http server
no ip domain-lookup
line con 0
 logging synchronous
```

```
    password cisco
    login
    transport input none
line aux 0
password cisco
 login
line vty 0 4
password cisco
 login
 !
end
copy run start
```

Save your file to the floppy disk so that you do not lose your work.

Select and copy all the lines, and return to your HyperTerminal session.

Normally, you would enter global configuration mode before pasting, but because you included the **conf t** command in your script, you don't have to.

If necessary, return to privileged EXEC mode. From the Edit menu, select Paste to Host.

After the past is complete, you have to confirm the copy operation.

Use **show run** to see if your configuration looks okay.

Using Notepad to Assist in Editing

Understanding how to use Notepad can save you from typing and typos during editing sessions. Carried to an extreme, you can do an entire router configuration in Notepad when you're at home or at the office and then paste it to the router's console when you get access. In the next steps, you look at a simple editing example.

Step 9

Configure the router with the following commands:

```
Router#config t
Router(config)#router rip
Router(config)#network 192.168.1.0
Router(config)#network 192.168.2.0
Router(config)#network 192.168.3.0
Router(config)#network 192.168.4.0
Router(config)#network 192.168.5.0
```

Press Ctrl+Z, and verify your configuration with **show run**. You just set up RIP to advertise a series of networks. But what if you want to change your routing protocol to IGRP? With the **no router rip** command, you easily get rid of RIP, but you would still have to retype the **network** commands. The next steps show you an alternative.

Step 10

Issue the **show run** command and hold the output so that the **router rip** commands are displayed. Using the keyboard or mouse, select the **router rip** command and all **network** statements.

Copy the selection.

Use the taskbar to return to Notepad.

Open a new document and paste the selection onto the blank page.

Step 11

In the new document, type the word **no** and a space in front of the word **router**.

Press the End key, and press Enter.

Type **router igrp 100** (but do not press Enter). The result should look like this:

```
no router rip
router igrp 100
 network 192.168.1.0
 network 192.168.2.0
 network 192.168.3.0
 network 192.168.4.0
 network 192.168.5.0
```

Step 12

Select your results and copy them.

Use the taskbar to return to your HyperTerminal session.

While in global configuration mode, paste the results.

Use the **show run** command to verify your configuration.

Reflection

How could using copy and paste with Notepad be helpful in other editing situations?

_____
_____
_____
_____
_____
_____
_____
_____
_____
_____
_____

Introductory Lab 2: Capturing HyperTerminal and Telnet Sessions

Objective

This activity describes how to capture HyperTerminal and Telnet sessions.

Note: Be sure to master these techniques. They save you a tremendous amount of typing in later labs and while working in the field.

Step 1

Log in to a router using HyperTerminal.

It is possible to capture the results of your HyperTerminal session in a text file, which can be viewed and/or printed using Notepad, WordPad, or Microsoft Word.

Note: This feature captures future screens, not what is currently onscreen. In essence, you are turning on a recording session.

To start a capture session, choose the menu option Transfer, Capture Text. The Capture Text dialog box appears, as shown in the figure.

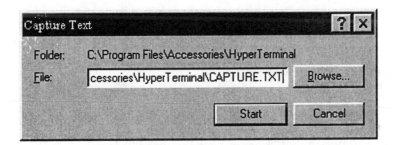

The default filename for a HyperTerminal capture is **CAPTURE.TXT**, and the default location of this file is C:\Program Files\Accessories\HyperTerminal.

Note: When you are using Telnet, the command to begin a capture (or log) is Terminal, Start Logging. The document you create has LOG as the extension. Other than the name and path of the capture file, the logging procedures are the same for both Telnet and HyperTerminal.

Make sure that your floppy disk is in the A: drive. When the Capture Text dialog box appears, change the File path to **A:\TestRun.txt**.

Click the Start button. Anything that appears onscreen after this point is copied to the file.

Step 2

Issue the **show run** command again, and view the entire configuration file.

From the Transfer menu, choose Capture Text, Stop.

Telnet users should select Stop Logging from the Terminal menu to end the session.

Step 3

Using the Start menu, launch Windows Explorer. You might find Windows Explorer under Programs or Accessories, depending on which version of Windows you use.

In the left pane, select the 3½ Floppy (A:) drive. On the right side, you should see the file you just created.

Double-click the TestRun.txt document's icon. The result should look something like this:

```
Router#show run
Building configuration...

Current configuration:
!
version 12.0
service timestamps debug uptime
service timestamps log uptime
no service password-encryption
!
hostname Router
!
enable secret 5 $1$HD2B$6iXb.h6QEJJjtn/NnwUHO.
!
!
ip subnet-zero
no ip domain-lookup
!
interface FastEthernet0/0
  --More--  _____        _____  no ip address
  no ip directed-broadcast
  shutdown
```

You may see gibberish that appears near the word "More". This is where you had to press the spacebar to see the rest of the list. You can use basic word-processing techniques to clean that up.

Suggestion

You should consider capturing each router configuration for every lab that you do. Capture files can be valuable as you review configuration features and prepare for certification exams.

Reflection

Could the capture techniques be useful if a member of your lab team misses a lab session? Can you use capture techniques to configure an off-site lab?

_____

_____

_____

_____

Introductory Lab 3: Access Control List Basics and Extended Ping

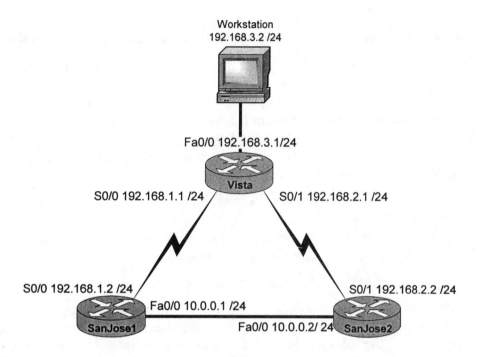

Objective

This lab activity reviews the basics of standard and extended access lists, which are used extensively in the CCNP curriculum.

Scenario

The LAN users connected to the Vista router are concerned about access to their network from hosts on network 10.0.0.0. You must use a standard access list to block all access to Vista's LAN from network 10.0.0.0/24.

You must also use an extended ACL to block network 192.168.3.0 host access to Web servers on the 10.0.0.0/24 network.

Step 1

Build and configure the network according to the diagram. Use RIPv1, and enable updates on all active interfaces with the appropriate **network** commands. The commands necessary to configure SanJose1 are shown here as an example:

```
SanJose1(config)#router rip
SanJose1(config-router)#network 192.168.1.0
SanJose1(config-router)#network 10.0.0.0
```

Use the **ping** command to verify your work and test connectivity between all interfaces.

Step 2

Check the routing table on Vista using the **show ip route** command. Vista should have all four networks in its table. Troubleshoot, if necessary.

Access Control List Basics

Access Control Lists (ACLs) are simple but powerful tools. When the access list is configured, each statement in the list is processed by the router in the order it was created. If an individual packet meets astatement's criteria, the permit or deny is applied to that packet, and no further list entries are checked. The next packet to be checked starts again at the top of the list.

It is not possible to reorder an access list, skip statements, edit statements, or delete statements from a numbered access list. With numbered access lists, any attempt to delete a single statement results in the entire list's deletion. Note that named ACLs (NACLs) do allow for deleting individual statements.

The following concepts apply to both standard and extended access lists:

Two-step process. First, the access list is created with one or more **access-list** commands while in global configuration mode. Second, the access list is applied by or referenced by other commands, such as the **access-group** command, to apply an ACL to an interface. An example would be the following:

```
Vista#config t
Vista(config)#access-list 50 deny 10.0.0.0 0.0.0.255
Vista(config)#access-list 50 permit any
Vista(config)#interface fastethernet 0/0
Vista(config-if)#ip access-group 50 out
Vista(config-if)#^Z
```

Syntax and Keywords

The basic syntax for creating an access list entry is as follows:

```
router(config)#access-list acl-number {permit | deny}...
```

The **permit** command allows packets matching the specified criteria to be accepted for whatever application the access list is being used for. The **deny** command discards packets matching the criteria on that line.

Two important keywords that can be used with IP addresses and the **access list** command are **any** and **host**. The keyword **any** matches all hosts on all networks (equivalent to **0.0.0.0 255.255.255.255**). The keyword **host** can be used with an IP address to indicate a single host address. The syntax is **host** *ip-address*, such as **host 192.168.1.10**. This is treated exactly the same as 192.168.1.10 0.0.0.0.

Implicit deny statement. Every access list contains a final "deny" statement that matches all packetsThis is called the implicit deny. Because the implicit deny statement is not visible in **show** command output, it is often overlooked, with dire consequences. As an example, consider the following single-line access list:

```
Router(config)#access-list 75 deny host 192.168.1.10
```

Access-list 75 clearly denies all traffic sourced from the host, 192.168.1.10. What might not be obvious is that all other traffic will be discarded as well, because the implicit **deny any** is the final statement in any access list.

At least one permit statement is required. There is no requirement that an ACL have a **deny** statement. If nothing else, the implicit **deny any** statement takes care of that. But if there are no **permit** statements, the effect will be the same as if there were only a single **deny any** statement.

Wildcard mask. In identifying IP addresses, ACLs use a wildcard mask instead of a subnet mask. Initially, they might look like the same thing, but closer observation reveals that they are very different. Remember that a binary 0 in a wildcard bitmask instructs the router to match the corresponding bit in the IP address.

In/out. When you are deciding whether an ACL should be applied to inbound or outbound traffic, always view things from the router's perspective. In other words, determine whether traffic is coming into the router (inbound) or leaving the router (outbound).

Applying ACLs. Extended ACLs should be applied as close to the source as possible, thereby conserving network resources. Standard ACLs (by necessity) must be applied as close to the destination as possible, because the standard ACL can match only at the source address of a packet.

Step 3

On router Vista, create the following standard ACL and apply it to the LAN interface:

```
Vista#config t
Vista(config)#access-list 50 deny 10.0.0.0 0.0.0.255
Vista(config)#access-list 50 permit any
Vista(config)#interface fastethernet 0/0
Vista(config-if)#ip access-group 50 out
Vista(config-if)#^Z
```

Try pinging 192.168.3.2 from SanJose1.

The ping should be successful. This result might be surprising, because you just blocked all traffic from the 10.0.0.0/8 network. The ping is successful because, even though it came from SanJose1, it is not sourced from the 10.0.0.0/8 network. A ping or traceroute from a router uses the closest interface to the destination as the source address. Thus, the ping is coming from the 192.168.1.0/24 (SanJose1's Serial 0/0).

In order to test the ACL from SanJose1, you must use the extended ping command to specify a specific source interface.

Step 4

On SanJose1, issue the following commands. Remember that the extended ping works only in privileged mode.

```
SanJose1#ping 192.168.3.2
Sending 5, 100-byte ICMP Echos to 192.168.3.2, timeout is 2 seconds:
!!!!!
Success rate is 100 percent (5/5), round-trip min/avg/max = 4/4/4 ms
SanJose1#
SanJose1#ping
Protocol [ip]:
Target IP address: 192.168.3.2
Repeat count [5]:
Datagram size [100]:
Timeout in seconds [2]:
Extended commands [n]: y
Source address or interface: 10.0.0.1
Type of service [0]:
Set DF bit in IP header? [no]:
Validate reply data? [no]:
Data pattern [0xABCD]:
Loose, Strict, Record, Timestamp, Verbose[none]:
Sweep range of sizes [n]:
Type escape sequence to abort.
Sending 5, 100-byte ICMP Echos to 192.168.3.2, timeout is 2 seconds:
.....
Success rate is 0 percent (0/5)
```

Step 5

Standard ACLs are numbered 1-99 (IOS 12 also allows standard lists to be numbered 1300–1699). Extended ACLs are numbered (IOS 12 allows 2000-2699). Extended ACLs can be used to enforce highly specific criteria for filtering packets. In this step, you will configure an extended ACL to block access to a Web server. Before you proceed, issue the **no access-list 50** and **no ip access-group 50** commands on the Vista router to remove the ACL configured previously.

First, you must configure both SanJose1 and SanJose 2 to act as Web servers, using the **ip http server** command, as shown:

```
SanJose1(config)#ip http server
```

```
SanJose2(config)#ip http server
```

From the workstation at 192.168.3.2, use a Web browser to view both routers' Web servers at 10.0.0.1 and 10.0.0.2. The Web login requires that you enter the router's enable secret password as the password.

After you verify Web connectivity between the workstation and the routers, proceed to Step 6.

Step 6

On the Vista router, enter the following commands:

```
Vista#access-list 101 deny tcp 192.168.3.0 0.0.0.255 10.0.0.0
        0.0.0.255 eq http
Vista#access-list 101 deny tcp 192.168.3.0 0.0.0.255 any eq ftp
Vista#access-list 101 permit any any
Vista#interface fastetherent 0/0
Vista#ip access-group 101 in
```

From the workstation at 192.168.3.2, again attempt to view the Web servers at 10.0.0.1 and 10.0.0.2. Both attempts should fail.

Next, browse SanJose1 at 192.168.1.2. Why isn't this blocked?

_____

Lab 1-1: Equal-Cost Load Balancing with RIP

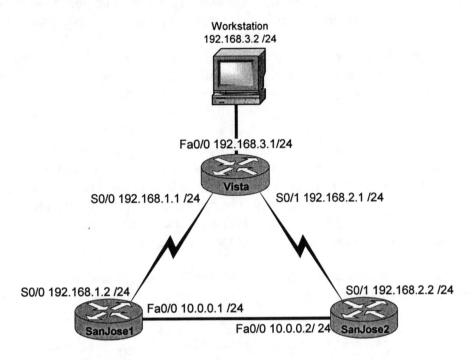

Objective

In this lab, you observe equal-cost load balancing on a per-packet and per-destination basis by using advanced debug commands.

Scenario

Vista has two paths to network 10.0.0.0. You must use advanced debug features to verify that both paths are being used to load-balance traffic to 10.0.0.0 and to test both per-packet and per-destination load balancing.

Step 1

Build and configure the network according to the diagram just shown. Use RIPv1 and enable updates on all active interfaces with network commands similar to these:

```
SanJose1(config)#router rip
SanJose1(config-router)#network 192.168.1.0
SanJose1(config-router)#network 10.0.0.0
```

Use the **ping** command to verify your work and test connectivity between all interfaces.

Step 2

Check the routing table on Vista using the **show ip route** command. Vista should have two routes to network 10.0.0.0 in its table. Troubleshoot, if necessary.

RIP automatically performs load balancing using equal-cost routes. Note that both routes have a metric (in this case, a hop count) of 1. RIP cannot perform unequal-cost load balancing. You will see (in the next lab) that IGRP can.

Step 3

To configure Vista to load-balance on a per-packet basis, both S0/0 and S0/1 must use *process switching*. Process switching forces the router to look in the routing table for the destination network of each routed packet. In contrast, *fast switching* performs a table lookup for the first packet only. The router then stores the result in a high-speed cache and uses the cached information to forward all additional packets to the same destination. Fast switching is the default setting.

Enable process switching on *both* of Vista's serial interfaces with the following interface configuration command:

```
Vista(config-if)#no ip route-cache
Verify that fast switching is disabled by using the show ip interface
command:
Vista#show ip interface s0/0
Serial0 is up, line protocol is up
  Internet address is 192.168.1.1 255.255.255.0
  Broadcast address is 255.255.255.255
  Address determined by non-volatile memory
  MTU is 1500 bytes
  Helper address is not set
  Directed broadcast forwarding is enabled
  Outgoing access list is not set
  Inbound  access list is not set
  Proxy ARP is enabled
  Security level is default
  Split horizon is enabled
  ICMP redirects are always sent
  ICMP unreachables are always sent
  ICMP mask replies are never sent
  IP fast switching is disabled
<output omitted>
```

Step 4

Because there are two routes to the destination network in the table, half the packets will be sent along one path, and half will travel over the other. The path selection alternates with each packet received. You can observe this process by using the **debug ip packet** command, which outputs information about IP packets sent and received by the router:

```
Vista#debug ip packet
```

With the debug running, send a few ping packets to 10.0.0.1 from your workstation at 192.168.3.2, and then return to Vista's console. As the pings are sent, the router outputs IP packet information. Stop the debug after a few successful pings using this command:

```
Vista#undebug all
```

Note: If you Telnetted to Vista, you probably will not see the debug output. To display the debug results during a Telnet session, you need to issue the **terminal monitor** command from privileged mode.

Examine the debug output. It can be a little confusing, because the ping requests and replies are mixed together. Look for a line of output that includes **d=10.0.0.1** (the destination address). On those lines, look for the interface that the packet was sent out on. The output interface should alternate between Serial0 and Serial1:

```
IP: s=192.168.3.2 (FastEthernet0), d=10.0.0.1 (Serial0/1),
        g=192.168.2.1, len 84, forward
IP: s=192.168.3.2 (FastEthernet0), d=10.0.0.1 (Serial0/1),
        g=192.168.1.1, len 84, forward
IP: s=192.168.3.2 (FastEthernet0), d=10.0.0.1 (Serial0/1),
        g=192.168.2.1, len 84, forward
IP: s=192.168.3.2 (FastEthernet0), d=10.0.0.1 (Serial0/0),
        g=192.168.1.1, len 84, forward
```

Step 5

You can also configure **debug** to output only the information you're interested in. To do this, you will configure an access control list (ACL) that **debug** will use to match packets against. Because you are interested in only the ping requests to the 10.0.0.0 network, you can create a list that filters everything else:

```
Vista(config)#access-list 101 permit icmp any 10.0.0.0 0.255.255.255
```

Enable debug with the following command:

```
Vista#debug ip packet 101
IP packet debugging is on for access list 101
```

Repeat the ping to 10.0.0.1 from your workstation, and return to Vista's console to view the output.

Step 6

After verifying per-packet load balancing, configure Vista to use per-destination load balancing. Both of Vista's serial interfaces must be configured to use fast switching so that the route cache can be used after the initial table lookup:

```
Vista(config-if)#ip route-cache
```

Use the **show ip interface** command to verify that fast switching is enabled.

Step 7

Because the routing table is consulted only once per destination, packets that are part of a train to a specific host all follow the same path. Only when a second destination forces another table lookup (or when the cached entry expires) is the alternate path used.

Use the **debug ip packet 101** command, and ping 10.0.0.1 from your workstation.

1. Which serial interface was the packet sent out on?

_____

Now ping 10.0.0.2.

2. Which serial interface was the packet sent out on?

_____

Although you won't get a reply, you can send pings to the phantom addresses 10.0.0.3 and 10.0.0.4 to see what path the router selects.

Finally, you can issue the **show ip cache** command to view the contents of the route cache. Note that mappings exist for 10.0.0.1 and 10.0.0.2, as well as for any other IP addresses you have recently pinged on the 10.0.0.0 network.

Note: Save your configuration. It can be used with the next lab.

Lab 1-2: Unequal-Cost Load Balancing with IGRP

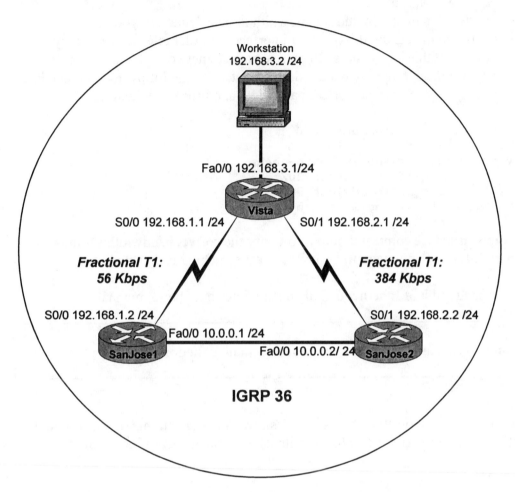

Objective

In this lab, you observe unequal-cost load balancing on an IGRP network by using advanced debug commands.

Scenario

Vista has two paths to network 10.0.0.0, but they have unequal IGRP metrics. You will configure unequal-cost load balancing and use advanced debug features to verify your work.

Step 1

Build and configure the network according to the diagram just shown. Use IGRP with an autonomous system number of 36, and enable updates on all active interfaces with these **network** commands:

```
SanJose2(config)#router igrp 36
SanJose2(config-router)#network 192.168.1.0
SanJose2(config-router)#network 10.0.0.0
```

Use ping to verify your work and test connectivity between all interfaces.

Also, because IGRP's metric includes bandwidth in its calculation, you must manually configure the bandwidth of serial interfaces in order to ensure accuracy. (For the purposes of this lab, Vista's alternative paths to network 10.0.0.0 aren't of unequal cost until the appropriate bandwidths are set.) Use the following commands to further configure Vista for the correct bandwidth and process switching:

```
Vista(config)#interface s0/0
Vista(config-if)#bandwidth 56
Vista(config-if)#no ip route-cache
Vista(config-if)#interface 20/1
Vista(config-if)#bandwidth 384
Vista(config-if)#no ip route-cache
```

Use the **show interface** command output to verify the correct bandwidth settings and the **show ip interface** command to ensure that fast switching is disabled.

1. Can the bandwidth of Ethernet or Token Ring interfaces be set manually?

2. Can an Ethernet interface be placed in fast switching mode?

Step 2

Check the routing table on Vista by using the **show ip route** command. Vista should have only one route to network 10.0.0.0 in its table. Troubleshoot if necessary.

Step 3

The variance value determines whether IGRP will accept unequal-cost routes. An IGRP router will only accept routes equal to the local best metric for the destination multiplied by the variance value. So, if an IGRP router's local best metric for Network A is 10476, and the variance is 3, the router will accept unequal-cost routes with any metric up to 31428 (10,476 x 3), as long as the advertising router is closer to the destination. An IGRP router accepts only up to four paths to the same network.

Note: An alternate route is added to the route table only if the next-hop router in that path is closer to the destination (has a lower metric value) than the current route.

By default, IGRP's variance is set to 1, which means that only routes that are exactly 1 times the local best metric are installed. Thus, a variance of 1 disables unequal-cost load balancing.

Configure Vista to enable unequal-cost load balancing using the following commands:

```
Vista(config)#router igrp 36
Vista(config-router)#variance 10
```

3. According to the help feature, what is the maximum variance value?

_____

Step 4

Check Vista's routing table again. Vista should have two routes to network 10.0.0.0 with unequal metrics.

4. What is the IGRP metric for the route to 10.0.0.0 via SanJose1?

_____

5. What is the IGRP metric for the route to 10.0.0.0 via SanJose2?

_____

Step 5

Now you can test unequal-cost load balancing by sending a ping packet to network 10.0.0.0 from Vista while debugging. First, configure an access list to restrict debug output to the ping requests from Vista to network 10.0.0.0:

```
Vista(config)#access-list 101 permit icmp any 10.0.0.0 0.255.255.255
```

Then, enable debug using the access list to filter output:

```
Vista(config)#debug ip packet 101
```

Finally, ping 10.0.0.1.

6. Are the packets load-balanced per destination or per packet?

_____

7. How is unequal-cost load balancing different from equal-cost load balancing?

_____

Lab 2-1: Configuring VLSM and IP Unnumbered

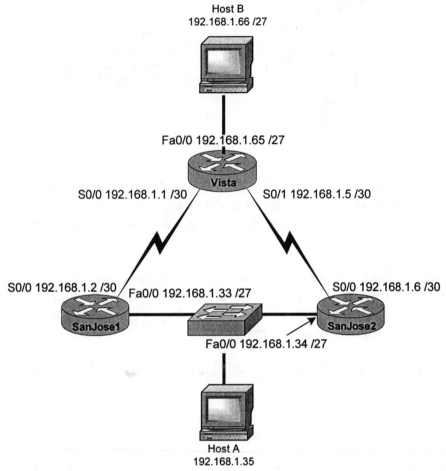

Host B
192.168.1.66 /27

Fa0/0 192.168.1.65 /27

Vista

S0/0 192.168.1.1 /30   S0/1 192.168.1.5 /30

S0/0 192.168.1.2 /30   Fa0/0 192.168.1.33 /27   S0/0 192.168.1.6 /30

SanJose1   SanJose2

Fa0/0 192.168.1.34 /27

Host A
192.168.1.35

Objective

In this lab, you configure VLSM and test its functionality with two different routing protocols, RIPv1 and RIPv2. Finally, you use IP unnumbered in place of VLSM to further conserve addresses.

Scenario

When International Travel Agency was much smaller, it wanted to configure its network using a single Class C address: 192.168.1.0 (shown in the figure). You are asked to configure the routers with the appropriate addresses. The company requires that at least 25 host addresses be available on each LAN, but it also demands that you conserve the maximum number of addresses for future growth.

To support 25 hosts on each subnet, a minimum of 5 bits is needed in the host portion of the address. 5 bits will yield 30 possible host addresses ($2^5 = 32 - 2$). If 5 bits must be used for hosts, the other 3 bits in the last octet can be added to the default 24-bit Class C mask. Thus, a 27-bit mask can be used to create the following subnets:

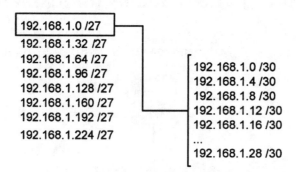

To maximize this address space, the 192.168.1.0 /27 subnet is subnetted further using a 30-bit mask. This creates subnets that can be used on point-to-point links with minimal waste, because each subnet can contain only two possible host addresses.

Step 1

Build and configure the network according to the diagram previously shown. This configuration requires the use of subnet 0, so you might need to enter the **ip subnet-zero** command, depending on which IOS version you are using. *Note:* Host A and Host B are not required to complete this lab.

On all three routers, configure RIPv1 and enable updates on all active interfaces with this network command:

```
SanJose1(config)#router rip
SanJose1(config-router)#network 192.168.1.0
```

Use **ping** to verify that each router can ping its directly connected neighbor. *Note:* Some remote networks might be unreachable. Despite this, proceed to Step 2.

Step 2

Issue the **show ip route** command on Vista, as shown in this example:

```
Vista#show ip route
<output omitted>
Gateway of last resort is not set

     192.168.1.0/24 is variably subnetted, 3 subnets, 2 masks
C        192.168.1.64/27 is directly connected, Ethernet0
C        192.168.1.0/30 is directly connected, Serial0
C        192.168.1.4/30 is directly connected, Serial1
```

The 192.168.1.32 /27 subnet is conspicuously absent from Vista's table.

1. The other routers also have incomplete tables. Why is this so?

Because you are using RIPv1 with VLSM, routing has broken down on your network. Remember that VLSM is not supported by classful routing protocols such as RIPv1 and IGRP. These protocols do not send subnet masks in their routing updates. In order for routing to work, you must configure RIPv2, which does support VLSM.

Step 3

At each of three router consoles, enable RIPv2 updates and turn off automatic route summarization, as shown in the following example:

```
SanJose1(config)#router rip
SanJose1(config-router)#version 2
SanJose1(config-router)#no auto-summary
```

When all three routers are running RIPv2, return to Vista and examine its routing table. It should now be complete, as shown here:

```
Vista#show ip route
<output omitted>

Gateway of last resort is not set

     192.168.1.0/24 is variably subnetted, 4 subnets, 2 masks
C       192.168.1.64/27 is directly connected, Ethernet0
R       192.168.1.32/27 [120/1] via 192.168.1.6, 00:00:12, Serial1
                        [120/1] via 192.168.1.2, 00:00:13, Serial0
C       192.168.1.0/30 is directly connected, Serial0
C       192.168.1.4/30 is directly connected, Serial1
```

Notice that Vista has received equal-cost routes to 192.168.1.32 /27 from both SanJose1 and SanJose2.

Step 4

Although VLSM has reduced ITA's address waste by creating very small subnets for point-to-point links, the IP unnumbered feature can obviate the need to address these links altogether. You further maximize ITA's address use by configuring IP unnumbered on every serial interface in the WAN. To configure IP unnumbered, use the following commands:

```
SanJose1(config)#interface serial 0/0
SanJose1(config-if)#ip unnumbered fastethernet 0/0

Vista(config)#interface serial 0/0
Vista(config-if)#ip unnumbered fastethernet 0/0
Vista(config-if)#interface serial 0/1
Vista(config-if)#ip unnumbered fastethernet 0/0

SanJose2(config)#interface serial 0/0
SanJose2(config-if)#ip unnumbered fastethernet 0/0
```

After your IP unnumbered configuration is complete, each serial interface borrows the address of the local LAN interface. Check Vista's table again:

```
Vista#show ip route
<output omitted>

Gateway of last resort is not set

     192.168.1.0/27 is subnetted, 2 subnets
C       192.168.1.64 is directly connected, Ethernet0
R       192.168.1.32 [120/1] via 192.168.1.34, 00:00:00, Serial1
                     [120/1] via 192.168.1.33, 00:00:08, Serial0
```

With IP unnumbered configured, only LANs require addresses. Because each LAN uses the same 27-bit mask, VLSM is not required, again making classful routing protocols, such as RIPv1 and IGRP, viable options.

Lab 2-2a: VLSM

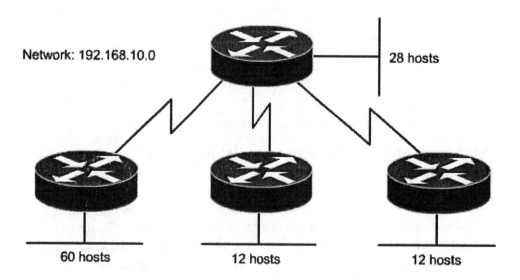

Network: 192.168.10.0   28 hosts

60 hosts   12 hosts   12 hosts

Objective

Create an addressing scheme using variable-length subnet masking (VLSM).

Scenario

You are assigned the Class C address 192.168.10.0 and must support the network shown in the diagram. You are not permitted to use IP unnumbered or NAT on this network. Create an addressing scheme that meets the requirements shown in the diagram.

_____
_____
_____
_____
_____

Lab 2-2b: VLSM

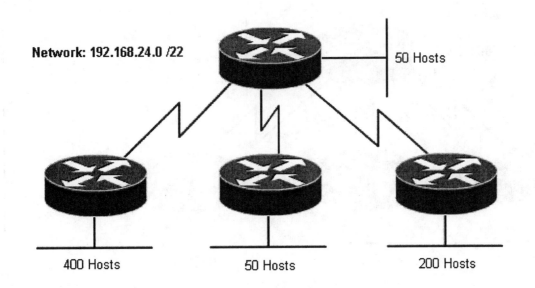

Network: 192.168.24.0 /22

50 Hosts

400 Hosts

50 Hosts

200 Hosts

Objective

Create an addressing scheme using VLSM.

Scenario

You are assigned the CIDR address 192.168.24.0 /22 and must support the network shown in the diagram. You are not permitted to use IP unnumbered or NAT on this network. Create an addressing scheme that meets the requirements shown in the diagram.

_____

_____

_____

_____

_____

Lab 2-2c: VLSM

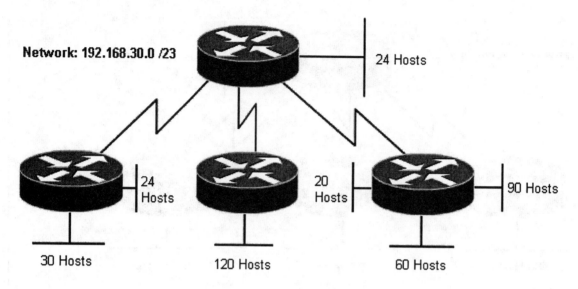

Network: 192.168.30.0 /23

24 Hosts

24 Hosts

20 Hosts

90 Hosts

30 Hosts

120 Hosts

60 Hosts

Objective

Create an addressing scheme using VLSM.

Scenario

You are assigned the CIDR address 192.168.30.0 /23 and must support the network shown in the diagram. You are not permitted to use IP unnumbered or NAT on this network. Create an addressing scheme that meets the requirements shown in the diagram.

Lab 2-3: Using DHCP and IP Helper Addresses

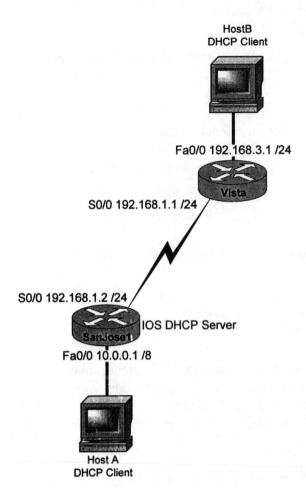

Objective

In this lab, you configure a Cisco router to act as a DHCP server for clients on two separate subnets. You also use the IP helper address feature to forward DHCP requests from a remote subnet.

Scenario

Clients on the 192.168.3.0/24 network and the 10.0.0.0/8 network require the services of DHCP for automatic IP configuration. You must configure SanJose1 to serve both subnets by creating two separate address pools. Finally, you need to configure Vista's E0 to forward UDP broadcasts (including DHCP requests) to SanJose1.

Step 1

Build and configure the network according to the diagram. Connect Host A and Host B as shown, but configure these clients to obtain their IP addresses automatically. Because these hosts rely on DHCP, you can't test them using **ping** until Step 5.

Configure RIPv2 on SanJose1 and Vista. Be sure to enable updates on all active interfaces with the **network** command:

```
SanJose1(config)#router rip
SanJose1(config)#version 2
SanJose1(config-router)#network 192.168.1.0
SanJose1(config-router)#network 10.0.0.0
```

Use **ping** and **show ip route** to verify your work and test connectivity between SanJose1 and Vista.

Step 2

Configure SanJose1 to act as a DHCP server for clients on the 10.0.0.0/8 network.

First, verify that SanJose1's software can use DHCP services and that they are enabled:

```
SanJose1(config)#service dhcp
```

Next, configure the DHCP address pool for the 10.0.0.0 network. Name the **pool 10-net**:

```
SanJose1(config)#ip dhcp pool 10-net
SanJose1(config-dhcp)#network 10.0.0.0 255.0.0.0
```

Step 3

International Travel Agency uses the first ten addresses in this address range to statically address servers and routers. From global configuration mode, you can exclude addresses from the DHCP pool so that the server does not attempt to assign them to clients. Configure SanJose1 to dynamically assign addresses from the ten-net pool, starting with 10.0.0.11:

```
SanJose1(config)#ip dhcp excluded-address 10.0.0.1 10.0.0.10
```

Step 4

Return to DHCP configuration mode and assign the following IP options: default gateway address, DNS server address, WINS server address, and domain name:

```
SanJose1(config-dhcp)#default-router 10.0.0.1
SanJose1(config-dhcp)#dns-server 10.0.0.3
SanJose1(config-dhcp)#netbios-name-server 10.0.0.4
SanJose1(config-dhcp)#domain-name xyz.net
```

Step 5

Now you are ready to test your DHCP server. Release and renew Host A's IP configuration.

Host A should be dynamically assigned the first available address in the pool, which is 10.0.0.11. Check Host A's configuration with **winipcfg** (or **ipconfig /all** for Windows NT and Windows 2000 users) to verify that it received the proper IP address, subnet mask, default gateway, domain name, DNS server address, and WINS server address. Troubleshoot, if necessary.

Step 6

Because Host B also requires dynamic IP configuration, create a second DHCP pool with address and gateway options appropriate to Host B's network, 192.168.3.0 /24:

```
SanJose1(config)#ip dhcp pool 192.168.3-net
SanJose1(dhcp-config)#network 192.168.3.0 255.255.255.0
SanJose1(dhcp-config)#default-router 192.168.3.1
SanJose1(dhcp-config)#dns-server 10.0.0.3
SanJose1(dhcp-config)#netbios-name-server 10.0.0.4
SanJose1(dhcp-config)#domain-name xyz.net
```

ITA has recently installed IP phones on the 192.168.3.0 network. These phones require a DHCP server to provide a TFTP server address (10.0.0.5). The Cisco IOS DHCP server configuration does not provide a keyword for TFTP servers, so you have to configure this option using its raw option number:

```
SanJose1(config-dhcp)#option 150 ip 10.0.0.5
```

Step 7

You have completed your configuration of the DHCP server. But Host B uses a UDP broadcast to find an IP address, and Vista is not configured to forward broadcasts. In order for DHCP to work, you must configure Vista's FastEthernet interface to forward UDP broadcasts to SanJose1:

```
Vista(config)#interface fastethernet 0/0
Vista(config-if)#ip helper-address 192.168.1.2
```

Step 8

Release and renew Host B's IP configuration while simultaneously logged into SanJose1's console (on a second host, if necessary).

1. Did SanJose1 report any DHCP messages?

_____

Verify, using **winipcfg** or **ipconfig /all**, that Host B received the correct IP configuration, and troubleshoot if necessary.

2. Because you didn't issue an **ip dhcp** *excluded-address* command, why didn't the DHCP server assign Host B 192.168.3.1?

_____

_____

_____

Issue **show ip dhcp ?** and note the choices. Try the **conflict** and **binding** options.

3. How did SanJose1 know to assign Host B an address from the 192.168.3-net pool and not the ten-net pool?

_____

_____

_____

Lab 3-1: Migrating from RIP to EIGRP

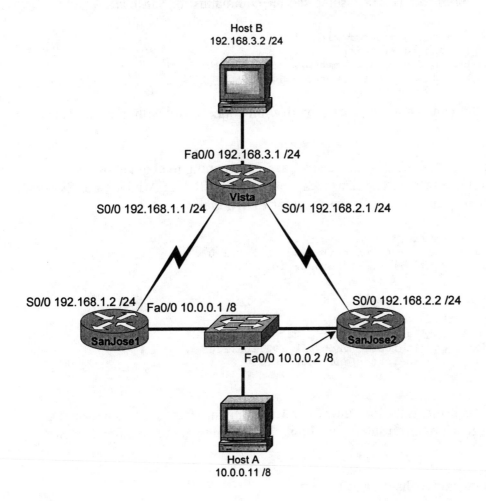

Host B
192.168.3.2 /24

Fa0/0 192.168.3.1 /24

Vista

S0/0 192.168.1.1 /24   S0/1 192.168.2.1 /24

S0/0 192.168.1.2 /24   Fa0/0 10.0.0.1 /8   S0/0 192.168.2.2 /24

SanJose1   SanJose2

Fa0/0 10.0.0.2 /8

Host A
10.0.0.11 /8

Objective

In this lab, you configure RIPv2 and then EIGRP so that you can compare their metric calculations.

Scenario

International Travel Agency (ITA) currently uses RIPv2 as its interior gateway protocol. You have been asked to migrate its network to EIGRP.

Step 1

Build and configure the network according to the diagram. *Note:* Host A and Host B are not required to complete this lab, but they might be used in testing or as Telnet clients.

On all three routers, configure RIPv2 and enable updates on all active interfaces with the **network** command. Here are some sample commands for SanJose1:

```
SanJose1(config)#router rip
SanJose1(config)#version 2
SanJose1(config-router)#network 192.168.1.0
SanJose1(config-router)#network 10.0.0.0
```

Use **ping** and **show ip route** to verify full connectivity within the network.

Step 2

As you migrate to EIGRP, you decide to leave RIP running to avoid a loss of connectivity. On SanJose1 and SanJose2, configure EIGRP for Autonomous System 24, as shown next. Do not configure Vista for EIGRP yet.

```
SanJose1(config)#router eigrp 24
SanJose1(config-router)#network 192.168.1.0
SanJose1(config-router)#network 10.0.0.0
```

and

```
SanJose2(config)#router eigrp 24
SanJose2(config-router)#network 192.168.2.0
SanJose2(config-router)#network 10.0.0.0
```

Step 3

From Vista's console, issue the **show ip route** command. Because you have not yet configured EIGRP on this router, you should have a route to the 10.0.0.0 /8 network via RIP.

1. What is the administrative distance of this route?

_____

2. What is the metric of this route?

_____

Enable debug so that changes to the routing table will be reported to the console.

```
SanJose1#debug ip routing
```

If you are connected via Telnet, you must also enter the **terminal monitor** command so that you can see the logging output.

Now enable EIGRP on Vista.

```
Vista(config)#router eigrp 24
Vista(config-router)#network 192.168.1.0
Vista(config-router)#network 192.168.2.0
Vista(config-router)#network 192.168.3.0
```

3. After you made this configuration, did debug report any changes to the routing table? If so, what were they?

_____

_____

Issue the **show ip route** command again from Vista. You should now have an EIGRP route to network 10.0.0.0 /8.

4. What is the metric of this route?

_____

5. Because this metric is higher than the metric of the RIP route, why did Vista choose the EIGRP route over the RIP route?

_____

_____

Step 4

To see more with the **debug ip routing** command, force the routing table to rebuild with this command:

```
Vista#clear ip route *
```

6. According to the debug output, what is the administrative distance of Vista's connected routes?

_____

7. What is the metric of the connected routes?

_____

Step 5

To complete the migration from RIP to EIGRP, you must disable RIP on all three routers. Be sure to turn off debug before exiting Vista:

```
Vista#undebug all
```

Lab 3-2: Configuring IGRP

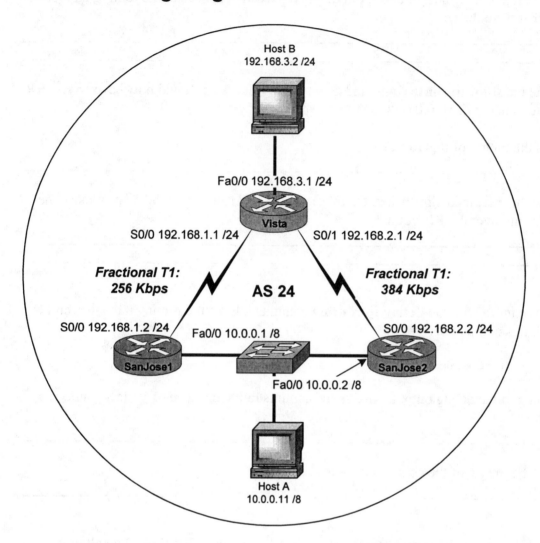

Objective

In this lab, you configure IGRP for unequal-cost load balancing and tune IGRP's timers to improve performance.

Scenario

International Travel Agency (ITA) asked you to implement IGRP in its WAN.

Step 1

Build and configure the network according to the diagram. *Note:* Host A and Host B are not required to complete this lab, but they might be used in testing or as Telnet clients.

On all three routers, configure IGRP for Autonomous System 24, and enable updates on all active interfaces with the **network** command. Configure unequal-cost load balancing using the **variance 5** command. Here are some sample commands for SanJose1:

```
SanJose1(config)#router igrp 24
SanJose1(config-router)#network 192.168.1.0
SanJose1(config-router)#network 10.0.0.0
SanJose1(config-router)#variance 5
```

Use **ping** and **show ip route** to verify full connectivity within the network.

Step 2

Because IGRP's metric includes bandwidth in its calculation, you must manually configure the bandwidth of serial interfaces in order for metrics to be accurate. Use the following commands to configure the correct bandwidth settings for each serial interface:

```
SanJose1(config)#interface serial 0/0
SanJose1(config-if)#bandwidth 256

Vista(config)#interface serial 0/0
Vista(config-if)#bandwidth 256
Vista(config-if)#interface serial 0/1
Vista(config-if)#bandwidth 384

SanJose2(config-if)#interface serial0/0
SanJose2(config-if)#bandwidth 384
```

Use the output from the **show interface** command to verify the correct bandwidth settings. Use the **show ip route** command to verify that the routers are installing two unequal-cost routes to the same destination:

```
Vista#show ip route
<output omitted>

I    10.0.0.0/8 [100/41072] via 192.168.1.2, 00:00:01, Serial0/0
                [100/28051] via 192.168.2.2, 00:00:00, Serial0/1
C    192.168.1.0/24 is directly connected, Serial0/0
C    192.168.2.0/24 is directly connected, Serial0/1
C    192.168.3.0/24 is directly connected, FastEthernet0/0
```

Step 3

On any of the routers, issue the **show ip protocols** command and check IGRP's invalid, holddown, and flush timers. *Note:* A route does not become invalid until after 270 seconds and is not flushed from the table until after more than 10 minutes (630 seconds). Also, the maximum hop count is set at 100 by default.

In small networks, it is advised that you adjust IGRP's timers to speed up the convergence process.

Fast IGRP is a specific set of timer settings that result in improved convergence. To set up Fast IGRP, you need to change the IGRP timers as follows: 15 seconds between updates, 45 seconds for route expiration, 0 seconds for holddown, and 60 seconds for flushing the route from the table. As part of this configuration, you must disable holddowns completely so that after the route for a given network has been removed, a new route for that destination network will be accepted immediately. Finally, you will reduce IGRP's maximum hop count to a number appropriate to ITA's network.

Configure Fast IGRP by issuing the following commands on all three routers:

```
SanJose1(config-router)#timers basic 15 45 0 60
SanJose1(config-router)#no metric holddown
SanJose1(config-router)#metric maximum-hops 10
```

Verify your settings with the **show ip protocols** command.

Step 4

In this step, you test your IGRP timer settings by simulating a link failure.

On SanJose1, enable debug so that any changes to the routing table will be reported to the console:

```
SanJose1#debug ip routing
```

If you are connected via Telnet, you must also enter the **terminal monitor** command so that you can see the logging output.

With your connection to SanJose1 open, log into Vista (on a separate workstation if necessary). On Vista, shut down the FastEthernet interface. This will cause the removal of 192.168.3.0 /24 from Vista's routing table.

```
Vista(config)#interface fastethernet0/0
Vista(config-if)#shutdown
```

Use the **show ip route** command to verify that Vista no longer possesses a route to 192.168.3.0 /24.

Return to SanJose1 and issue the **show ip route** command. Note: The route to 192.168.3.0 is still in SanJose1's table, but it is flagged as possibly down.

1. How long will you have to wait before this route is removed?

To check your answer, wait for the debug output on SanJose1 to report that the route to 192.168.3.0 has been flushed.

2. If SanJose1 had been configured with default timers, how long would it have taken for the route to be flushed?

Lab 3-3: Configuring Default Routing with RIP and IGRP

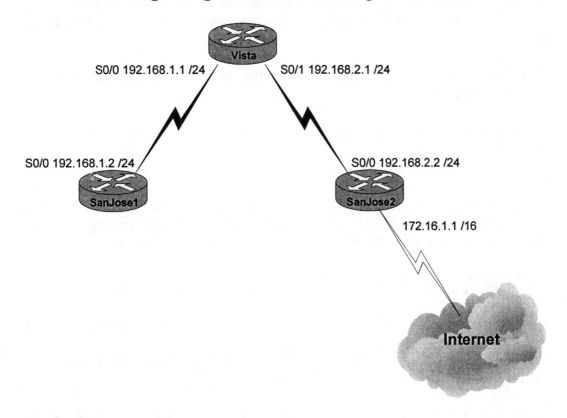

Objective

In this lab, you configure a default route and use RIP to propagate this default information to other routers. When you have this configuration working, you must migrate the network from RIP to IGRP and configure default routing to work with that protocol as well.

Scenario

International Travel Agency (ITA) asked you to configure default routing for its network, which currently uses RIP. The company connects to the Internet via SanJose2, so you decide to configure a static default route on that router. Then you must configure RIP so that it will propagate the default route to the other RIP routers.

ITA also asked you to explore the possibility of migrating all routers to IGRP. As a test, you must configure the three routers in this scenario for IGRP and configure default routing for that protocol as well.

Procedures

Before you begin this lab, it is recommended that you reload each router after erasing its startup configuration. This prevents problems caused by residual configurations. After you prepare the equipment, proceed with Step 1.

Step 1

Build and configure the network according to the diagram. Do not configure the 172.16.1.1/16 address on SanJose2 yet. This network connects ITA to its ISP and the Internet.

On all three routers, configure RIP, but be sure not to configure SanJose2's RIP process to include the 172.16.0.0/16 network.

Use **ping** and **show ip route** to verify full connectivity within the network, excluding 172.16.0.0/16.

Step 2

Configure SanJose2 to simulate the existence of an outside network. For this scenario, you need to simulate the link between ITA and its provider by configuring a loopback address with an IP address. Enter the following commands on SanJose2:

```
SanJose2(config)#interface loopback0
SanJose2(config-if)#ip address 172.16.1.1 255.255.255.0
```

Note: If you ping 172.16.1.1 from SanJose2's console, the loopback interface replies.

From Vista's console, attempt to ping 172.16.1.1. This ping should fail, because the 172.16.0.0/16 network is not in Vista's table.

1. If no default route exists, what does a router do with a packet destined for a network that is not in its table?

Step 3

Next, you must configure SanJose2 with a 0.0.0.0/0 default route pointed at the simulated ISP. Issue the following command on SanJose2:

```
SanJose2(config)#ip route 0.0.0.0 0.0.0.0 loopback0
```

This command statically configures the default route, which will direct traffic out the simulated WAN link (loopback 0).

RIP automatically propagates statically defined default routes, unless you are using IOS version 12.1. So, depending on your IOS version, you might need to explicitly configure RIP to propagate this 0.0.0.0/0 route. Enter these commands on SanJose2:

```
SanJose2(config)#router rip
SanJose2(config-router)#default-information originate
```

Step 4

Now check the routing tables of SanJose1 and Vista using the **show ip route** command. Verify that they both have received and installed a route to 0.0.0.0/0 in their tables.

2. On Vista, what is the metric of this route?

3. On SanJose1, what is the metric of this route?

SanJose1 and Vista still don't have routes to 172.16.0.0/16 in their tables. From Vista, ping 172.16.1.1. This ping should be successful.

4. Why does the ping to 172.16.1.1 work, even though there is no route to 172.16.0.0/16 in Vista's table?

Check to be sure that SanJose2 can also ping 172.16.1.1. Troubleshoot, if necessary.

Step 5

With default routing now working, you must migrate the network from RIP to IGRP for testing purposes. Issue the following command on all three routers:

```
SanJose1(config)#no router rip
```

With RIP removed from each router's configuration, configure IGRP on all three routers using AS 24, as shown:

```
SanJose1(config)#router igrp 24
SanJose1(config-router)#network 192.168.1.0
...
Vista(config)#router igrp 24
Vista(config-router)#network 192.168.1.0
Vista(config-router)#network 192.168.2.0
...
SanJose2(config)#router igrp 24
SanJose2(config-router)#network 192.168.2.0
```

Use **ping** and **show ip route** to verify that IGRP is working properly. Don't worry about the 172.16.1.1 loopback address on SanJose2 yet.

Step 6

Check SanJose2's routing table. The static default route to 0.0.0.0/0 should still be there. To propagate this route with RIP, you issued the **default-information originate** command. (Depending on your IOS version, you might not have needed to do that.) The **default-information originate** command is not available in an IGRP configuration. Thus, you must use a different method to propagate default information in IGRP.

On SanJose2, issue the following commands:

```
SanJose2(config)#router igrp 24
SanJose2(config-router)#network 172.16.0.0
SanJose2(config-router)#exit
SanJose2(config)#ip default-network 172.16.0.0
```

These commands configure IGRP to update its neighbor routers about the network 172.16.0.0/16, which includes your simulated ISP link (loopback 0). Not only will IGRP advertise this network, but the **ip default-network** command also will flag this network as a candidate default route (denoted by an asterisk in the routing table). When a network is flagged as a default, that flag stays with the route as it passed from neighbor to neighbor by IGRP.

Check the routing tables of SanJose1 and Vista. If they don't yet have the 172.16.0.0/16 route with an asterisk, you might need to wait for another IGRP update (90 seconds). You can also issue the **clear ip route *** command on all three routers if you want to force them to immediately send new updates.

When the 172.16.0.0/16 route appears as a candidate default in all three routing tables, proceed to the next step.

Step 7

Because the 172.16.0.0/16 network is known explicitly by SanJose1 and Vista, you need to create a second loopback interface on SanJose2 to test your default route. Issue the following commands on SanJose2:

```
SanJose2(config)#interface loopback1
SanJose2(config-if)#ip address 10.0.0.1 255.0.0.0
```

This loopback interface simulates another external network.

Return to SanJose1 and check its routing table using the **show ip route** command.

5. Is there a route to the 10.0.0.0/8 network?

_____

From SanJose1, ping 10.0.0.1. This ping should be successful.

6. If there is no route to 10.0.0.0/8 and no route to 0.0.0.0/0, why does this ping succeed?

_____

Lab 3-4: Configuring Floating Static Routes

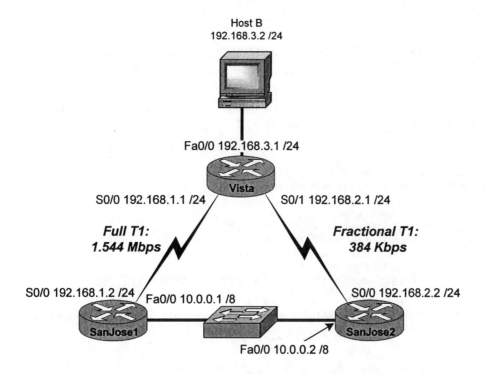

Objective

In this lab, you configure a floating static route.

Scenario

International Travel Agency (ITA) uses a combination of static routing and RIP in the core of its network. One of ITA's key boundary routers, Vista, has two routes to the 10.0.0.0/8 network, but only one of these routes is advertised by RIP. If you configure the other path statically, using the default administrative distance, the static route will be preferred over the RIP route. However, ITA wants the RIP route to be preferred, because it has higher bandwidth. Therefore, you must override the default administrative distance of the static route to create a floating static route.

Procedures

Before you begin this lab, it is recommended that you reload each router after erasing its startup configuration. This prevents problems caused by residual configurations. After you have prepared the equipment, proceed with Step 1.

Step 1

Build and configure the network according to the diagram. Be sure to configure Host B. Do not configure a routing protocol.

Use ping to verify that directly connected link partners can reach each other.

Step 2

Configure routing on the three routers. SanJose1 and Vista will run RIP, so issue the following commands on the appropriate router:

```
SanJose1(config)#router rip
SanJose1(config-router)#network 192.168.1.0
SanJose1(config-router)#network 10.0.0.0
...
Vista(config)#router rip
Vista(config-router)#network 192.168.1.0
Vista(config-router)#network 192.168.3.0
SanJose2 will reach Vista using a static route. Enter the following
        command on SanJose2:
SanJose2(config)#ip route 192.168.3.0 255.255.255.0 192.168.2.1
```

Verify that Host B can ping the serial interfaces of both SanJose1 (192.168.1.2) and SanJose2 (192.168.2.2). Troubleshoot, if necessary.

Step 3

Check Vista's routing table. It should have a route to the 10.0.0.0/8 network.

1. Which interface will Vista use to reach the 10.0.0.0/8 network?

_____

Now that you verified that the RIP route to the 10.0.0.0/8 network is operational, configure a static route on Vista that will use SanJose2 to get to 10.0.0.0/8, using the following command:

```
Vista(config)#ip route 10.0.0.0 255.0.0.0 192.168.2.2
```

When you have configured Vista with this static route, check its routing table using the **show ip route** command. Only the static route to the 10.0.0.0/8 network should be in Vista's table.

2. What happened to the RIP route?

_____

Remember that ITA wants you to configure Vista to use the SanJose2 link to 10.0.0.0/8 only if the other route goes down. Thus, you must reconfigure the static route on Vista so that it floats; that is, it remains in the configuration but is not installed in the routing table until a route with a better metric is lost.

Before you configure a floating static route on Vista, you must remove the first static route using the following command:

```
Vista(config)#no ip route 10.0.0.0 255.0.0.0 192.168.2.2
```

When you have verified that this static route is no longer part of Vista's configuration, issue the following command to create a floating static route:

```
Vista(config)#ip route 10.0.0.0 255.0.0.0 192.168.2.2 130
```

The 130 at the end of this command overrides the default administrative distance for a static route. By default, a static route has an administrative distance of 1. In this scenario, you must increase the administrative distance so that it is higher than RIP's administrative distance of 120. That way, the RIP route will be preferred. Vista will install the static route only if the RIP route fails.

As an extra precaution in case the link between SanJose1 and Vista should fail, add the following floating static route to SanJose1:

```
SanJose1(config)#ip route 192.168.3.0 255.255.255.0 10.0.0.2 130
```

Step 4

After you reconfigure the static route to be a floating static route, check Vista's routing table again. Now, only the RIP route to 10.0.0.0/8 should be in the table. Verify that routing is working by pinging Host A (10.0.0.11) from Host B. Troubleshoot, if necessary.

Although you can't see your floating static route in Vista's table, it remains in the configuration file. You can observe how Vista reacts to a link failure by issuing the following command:

```
Vista#debug ip routing
```

Now verify that you have configured the routers correctly, and disconnect SanJose1's Ethernet connection to the 10.0.0.0/8 network. You might have to wait a few seconds, but eventually the debug output on Vista should notify you of the change:

```
RT: del 10.0.0.0 via 192.168.1.2, rip metric [120/1]
RT: delete network route to 10.0.0.0
RT: add 10.0.0.0/8 via 192.168.2.2, static metric [130/0]
```

Check Vista's routing table to ensure that the static route has been installed. As a final test, ping 10.0.0.1 and 10.0.0.2 from Host B. These pings should be successful. Troubleshoot, if necessary.

Lab 4-1: Configuring OSPF

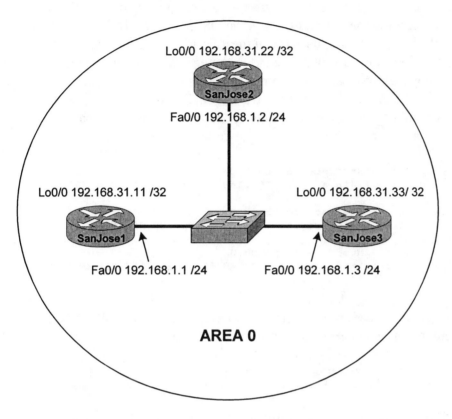

Objective

In this lab, you configure OSPF on three Cisco routers. First, you configure loopback interfaces to provide stable OSPF Router IDs. Then you configure the OSPF process and enable OSPF on the appropriate interfaces. After OSPF is enabled, you tune the update timers and configure authentication.

Scenario

The backbone of International Travel Agency's (ITA) WAN, located in San Jose, consists of three routers connected via an Ethernet core. You must configure these core routers as members of OSPF Area 0. Because the core routers are connected to the Internet, you decide to implement security, preventing unauthorized routers from joining Area 0. Also, within the core, you want network failures to be realized quickly.

Step 1

Build and configure the network according to the diagram, but do not configure OSPF yet. A switch or hub is required to connect the three routers via Ethernet.

Use **ping** to verify your work and test connectivity between the FastEthernet interfaces.

Step 2

On each router, configure a loopback interface with a unique IP address. Cisco routers use the highest loopback IP address as the OSPF Router ID. In the absence of a loopback interface, the router uses the highest IP address among its active interfaces, which might force a router to change router IDs if an interface goes down. Because loopback interfaces are immune to physical and data-link problems, they should be used to derive the router ID. To avoid conflicts with registered network addresses, use private network ranges for your loopback interfaces. Configure your core routers using the following commands:

```
SanJose1(config)#interface loopback 0
SanJose1(config-if)#ip address 192.168.31.11 255.255.255.255

SanJose2(config)#interface loopback 0
SanJose2(config-if)#ip address 192.168.31.22 255.255.255.255

SanJose3(config)#interface loopback 0
SanJose3(config-if)#ip address 192.168.31.33 255.255.255.255
```

Step 3

Now that loopback interfaces are configured, you must configure OSPF. Use the following commands as an example to configure each router:

```
SanJose1(config)#router ospf 1
SanJose1(config-router)#network 192.168.1.0 0.0.0.255 area 0
```

Note: An OSPF process ID is locally significant; it does not need to match neighboring routers. The ID is needed to identify a unique instance of an OSPF database, because multiple processes can run concurrently on a single router.

Step 4

After you enable OSPF routing on each of the three routers, verify its operation using **show** commands. Several important **show** commands can be used to gather OSPF information. First, issue the **show ip protocols** command on any of the three routers, as shown here:

```
SanJose1#show ip protocols
Routing Protocol is "ospf 1"
  Sending updates every 0 seconds
  Invalid after 0 seconds, hold down 0, flushed after 0
  Outgoing update filter list for all interfaces is
  Incoming update filter list for all interfaces is
  Redistributing: ospf 1
  Routing for Networks:
    192.168.1.0
  Routing Information Sources:
    Gateway         Distance        Last Update
  Distance: (default is 110)
```

Note: The update timers are set to 0. Updates are not sent at regular intervals; they are event-driven. Next, use the **show ip ospf** command to get more details about the OSPF process, including the router ID:

```
SanJose1#show ip ospf
 Routing Process "ospf 1" with ID 192.168.31.11
 Supports only single TOS(TOS0) routes
 SPF schedule delay 5 secs, Hold time between two SPFs 10 secs
 Minimum LSA interval 5 secs. Minimum LSA arrival 1 secs
 Number of external LSA 0. Checksum Sum 0x0
 Number of DCbitless external LSA 0
 Number of DoNotAge external LSA 0
 Number of areas in this router is 1. 1 normal 0 stub 0 nssa
 External flood list length 0
    Area BACKBONE(0)
        Number of interfaces in this area is 1
        Area has no authentication
        SPF algorithm executed 5 times
        Area ranges are
        Number of LSA 4. Checksum Sum 0x1CAC4
        Number of DCbitless LSA 0
        Number of indication LSA 0
        Number of DoNotAge LSA 0
        Flood list length 0
```

1. What address is your router using as its router ID?

_____

You should see the loopback interface as the router ID. To see your OSPF neighbors, use the **show ip ospf neighbor** command. The output of this command displays all known OSPF neighbors, including their router IDs, their interface addresses, and their adjacency status. Also issue the **show ip ospf neighbor detail** command, which outputs even more information:

```
SanJose1#show ip ospf neighbor
Neighbor ID     Pri    State          Dead Time    Address
        Interface
192.168.31.22    1     FULL/BDR       00:00:36     192.168.1.2
        FastEthernet0/0
192.168.31.33    1     FULL/DR        00:00:33     192.168.1.3
        FastEthernet0/0

SanJose1#show ip ospf neighbor detail
 Neighbor 192.168.31.22, interface address 192.168.1.2
    In the area 0 via interface FastEthernet0/0
    Neighbor priority is 1, State is FULL, 6 state changes
    DR is 192.168.1.3 BDR is 192.168.1.2
    Options 2
    Dead timer due in 00:00:34
    Index 2/2, retransmission queue length 0, number of
      retransmission 2
    First 0x0(0)/0x0(0) Next 0x0(0)/0x0(0)
    Last retransmission scan length is 1, maximum is 1
    Last retransmission scan time is 0 msec, maximum is 0 msec
 Neighbor 192.168.31.33, interface address 192.168.1.3
    In the area 0 via interface FastEthernet0/0
    Neighbor priority is 1, State is FULL, 6 state changes
    DR is 192.168.1.3 BDR is 192.168.1.2
```

```
Options 2
Dead timer due in 00:00:30
Index 1/1, retransmission queue length 0, number of
    retransmission 1
First 0x0(0)/0x0(0) Next 0x0(0)/0x0(0)
Last retransmission scan length is 1, maximum is 1
Last retransmission scan time is 0 msec, maximum is 0 msec
```

2. Based on the output of this command, which router is the Designated Router (DR) on this network?

_____

3. Which router is the Backup Designated Router (BDR)?

_____

Most likely, the router with the highest router ID is the DR, the router with the second-highest router ID is the BDR, and the other router is a DRother.

Because each interface on a given router is connected to a different network, some of the key OSPF information is interface-specific. Issue the **show ip ospf interface** command for your router's FastEthernet interface as shown here:

```
SanJose1#show ip ospf interface fa0/0
FastEthernet0/0 is up, line protocol is up
  Internet Address 192.168.1.1/24, Area 0
  Process ID 1, Router ID 192.168.31.11, Network Type BROADCAST,
      Cost: 1
  Transmit Delay is 1 sec, State DROTHER, Priority 1
  Designated Router (ID) 192.168.31.33, Interface address
      192.168.1.3
  Backup Designated router (ID) 192.168.31.22, Interface address
      192.168.1.2
  Timer intervals configured, Hello 10, Dead 40, Wait 40,
      Retransmit 5
    Hello due in 00:00:09
  Index 1/1, flood queue length 0
  Next 0x0(0)/0x0(0)
  Last flood scan length is 0, maximum is 1
  Last flood scan time is 0 msec, maximum is 0 msec
  Neighbor Count is 2, Adjacent neighbor count is 2
    Adjacent with neighbor 192.168.31.22  (Backup Designated
        Router)
    Adjacent with neighbor 192.168.31.33  (Designated Router)
  Suppress hello for 0 neighbor(s)
```

4. Based on the output of this command, what OSPF network type is your router's Ethernet interface connected to?

_____

5. What is the Hello update timer set to?

_____

6. What is the Dead timer set to?

_____

Ethernet networks are known to OSPF as broadcast networks. The default timer values are 10-second hello updates and 40-second dead intervals.

Step 5

You decide to adjust OSPF timers so that the core routers will detect network failures in less time. This will increase traffic, but this is less of a concern on your high-speed core Ethernet segment than on a busy WAN link. You decide the need for quick convergence at the core outweighs the extra traffic. Manually change the Hello and Dead intervals on SanJose1:

```
SanJose1(config)#interface fastethernet 0/0
SanJose1(config-if)#ip ospf hello-interval 5
SanJose1(config-if)#ip ospf dead-interval 20
```

These commands set the Hello update timer to 5 seconds and the Dead interval to 20 seconds. Although the Cisco IOS does not require it, you should configure the Dead interval to four times the Hello interval. This ensures that routers experiencing temporary link problems can recover and are not declared dead unnecessarily, causing a ripple of updates and recalculations throughout the internetwork.

After you change timers on SanJose1, issue the **show ip ospf neighbor** command.

7. Does SanJose1 still show that it has OSPF neighbors?

To find out what happened to SanJose1's neighbors, use the IOS debug feature. Enter the command **debug ip ospf events**.

```
SanJose1#debug ip ospf events
OSPF events debugging is on
SanJose1#
00:08:25: OSPF: Rcv hello from 192.168.31.22 area 0 from
        FastEthernet0/0 192.168.1.2
00:08:25: OSPF: Mismatched hello parameters from 192.168.1.2
00:08:25: Dead R 40 C 20, Hello R 10 C 5  Mask R 255.255.255.0
        C 255.255.255.0
SanJose1#
00:08:32: OSPF: Rcv hello from 192.168.31.33 area 0 from
        FastEthernet0/0 192.168.1.3
00:08:32: OSPF: Mismatched hello parameters from 192.168.1.3
00:08:32: Dead R 40 C 20, Hello R 10 C 5  Mask R 255.255.255.0
        C 255.255.255.0
```

8. According to the **debug** output, what is preventing SanJose1 from forming relationships with the other two OSPF routers in Area 0?

The Hello and Dead intervals must be the same before routers within an area can form neighbor adjacencies.

Turn off debug using **undebug all**, or just **u all**.

```
SanJose1#undebug all
All possible debugging has been turned off
```

The Hello and Dead intervals are declared in Hello packet headers. In order for OSPF routers to establish a relationship, their Hello and Dead intervals must match.

Configure the SanJose2 and SanJose3 Hello and Dead timers to match the timers on SanJose1. Before you continue, verify that these routers can now communicate by checking the OSPF neighbor table.

Step 6

Whether intentional, or by accident, you do not want any unauthorized routers exchanging updates within Area 0. You accomplish this by adding encrypted authentication to each OSPF packet header. You select message digest (MD5) authentication. This mode of authentication sends a message digest, or hash, in place of the password. OSPF neighbors must be configured with the same message digest key number, encryption type, and password in order to authenticate using the hash.

To configure a message digest password for SanJose1 to use on its Ethernet interface, use these commands:

```
SanJose1(config)#interface fastethernet 0/0
SanJose1(config-if)#ip ospf message-digest-key 1 md5 7 itsasecret
SanJose1(config-if)#router ospf 1
SanJose1(config-router)#area 0 authentication message-digest
```

After you enter these commands, wait 20 seconds, and then issue the **show ip ospf neighbor** command on SanJose1.

9. Does SanJose1 still show that it has OSPF neighbors?

Use the **debug ip ospf events** command to determine why SanJose1 does not see its neighbors:

```
SanJose1#debug ip ospf events
OSPF events debugging is on
SanJose1#
00:49:32: OSPF: Send with youngest Key 1
SanJose1#
00:49:33: OSPF: Rcv pkt from 192.168.31.33, FastEthernet0/0 :
        Mismatch Authentication type. Input packet specified type
        0, we use type 2
00:49:33: OSPF: Rcv pkt from 192.168.31.22, FastEthernet0/0 :
        Mismatch Authentication type. Input packet specified type ,
        we use type 2
SanJose1#u all
All possible debugging has been turned off
```

Again, you see that OSPF routers will not communicate unless certain configurations match. In this case, the routers are not communicating because the authentication fields in the OSPF packet header are different.

Correct this problem by configuring authentication on the other two routers. Remember that you must use the same key number, encryption type, and password on each router.

After your configurations are complete, verify that the routers can communicate by using the **show ip ospf neighbors** command.

```
SanJose1#show ip ospf neighbors
Neighbor ID      Pri   State          Dead Time    Address
     Interface
192.168.31.33     1    FULL/DR        00:00:16     192.168.1.3
     FastEthernet0/0
192.168.31.22     1    FULL/BDR       00:00:15     192.168.1.2
     FastEthernet0/0
```

Step 7

Save your configurations to NVRAM. They will be used to begin the next lab. At the conclusion of each lab, it is recommended that you copy and save each router's configuration file for future reference.

Lab 4-2: Examining the DR/BDR Election Process

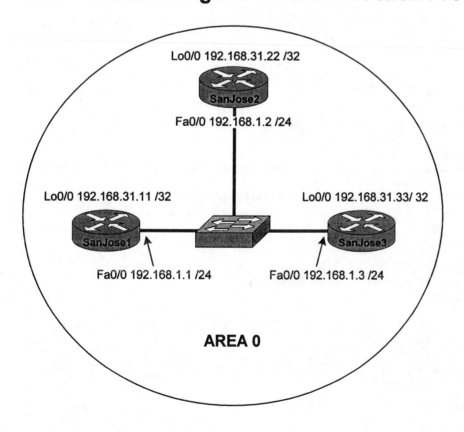

Objective

In this lab, you observe the OSPF DR and BDR election process using **debug** commands. Then you assign each OSPF interface a priority value to force the election of a specific router as a DR.

Scenario

The backbone of International Travel Agency's enterprise network consists of three routers connected via an Ethernet core. SanJose1 has more memory and processing power than the other core routers. Unfortunately, other core routers are continually elected as the DR under the default settings. In the interest of optimization, you want to ensure that SanJose1 is elected the DR, because it is best suited to handle associated extra duties, including management of Link State Advertisements (LSA) for Area 0. You decide to investigate and correct the situation.

Step 1

Build and configure the network according to the diagram. Configure OSPF on all Ethernet interfaces. A switch or hub is required to connect the three routers via Ethernet. Be sure to configure each router with the loopback interface and IP address shown in the diagram.

Use **ping** to verify your work and test connectivity between the Ethernet interfaces.

Step 2

Use the **show ip ospf neighbor detail** command to verify that the OSPF routers have formed adjacencies:

```
SanJose3#show ip ospf neighbor detail
Neighbor 192.168.31.11, interface address 192.168.1.1
    In the area 0 via interface FastEthernet0/0
    Neighbor priority is 1, State is FULL, 12 state changes
    DR is 192.168.1.3 BDR is 192.168.1.2
    Options 2
    Dead timer due in 00:00:17
    Index 2/2, retransmission queue length 0, number of
        retransmission 1
    First 0x0(0)/0x0(0) Next 0x0(0)/0x0(0)
    Last retransmission scan length is 1, maximum is 1
    Last retransmission scan time is 0 msec, maximum is 0 msec
Neighbor 192.168.31.22, interface address 192.168.1.2
    In the area 0 via interface FastEthernet0/0
    Neighbor priority is 1, State is FULL, 6 state changes
    DR is 192.168.1.3 BDR is 192.168.1.2
    Options 2
    Dead timer due in 00:00:15
    Index 1/1, retransmission queue length 0, number of
        retransmission 5
    First 0x0(0)/0x0(0) Next 0x0(0)/0x0(0)
    Last retransmission scan length is 1, maximum is 1
    Last retransmission scan time is 0 msec, maximum is 0 msec
```

1. Which router is the DR? Why?

_____

2. Which router is the BDR? Why?

_____

Recall that router IDs determine the DR and BDR.

Step 3

If your network is configured according to the diagram, SanJose1 will not be the DR. You decide to temporarily shut down SanJose3, which has the highest router ID (192.168.31.33), and observe the DR/BDR election process. To observe the election, issue the following **debug** command on SanJose1:

```
SanJose1#debug ip ospf adj
```

Now that OSPF adjacency events will be logged to SanJose1's console, you can remove SanJose3 from the OSPF network by shutting down its FastEthernet interface:

```
SanJose3(config)#interface fastethernet 0/0
SanJose3(config-if)#shutdown
Watch the debug output on SanJose1:
SanJose1#
00:48:47: OSPF: Rcv hello from 192.168.31.22 area 0 from
        FastEthernet0/0 192.168.1.2
00:48:47: OSPF: Neighbor change Event on interface FastEthernet0/0
00:48:47: OSPF: DR/BDR election on FastEthernet0/0
00:48:47: OSPF: Elect BDR 192.168.31.11
00:48:47: OSPF: Elect DR 192.168.31.22
00:48:47: OSPF: Elect BDR 192.168.31.11
00:48:47: OSPF: Elect DR 192.168.31.22
00:48:47:        DR: 192.168.31.22 (Id)    BDR: 192.168.31.11 (Id)
00:48:47: OSPF: Remember old DR 192.168.31.33 (id)
00:48:47: OSPF: End of hello processing
```

3. Who is elected DR? Why?

_____

The former BDR is promoted to DR.

In the debug output, look for a statement about remembering the "old DR." Unless SanJose1 and SanJose2 are powered off, they will remember that SanJose3 was the old DR. When SanJose3 comes back online, these routers will allow SanJose3 to reassume its role as DR:

```
SanJose1#
00:51:32: OSPF: Rcv hello from 192.168.31.22 area 0 from
        FastEthernet0/0 192.168.1.2
00:51:32: OSPF: End of hello processing
00:51:33: OSPF: Rcv hello from 192.168.31.33 area 0 from
        FastEthernet0/0 192.168.1.3
```

```
00:51:33: OSPF: 2 Way Communication to 192.168.31.33 on
        FastEthernet0/0, state 2WAY
00:51:33: OSPF: Neighbor change Event on interface FastEthernet0/0
00:51:33: OSPF: DR/BDR election on FastEthernet0/0
00:51:33: OSPF: Elect BDR 192.168.31.11
00:51:33: OSPF: Elect DR 192.168.31.33
00:51:33:        DR: 192.168.31.33 (Id)   BDR: 192.168.31.11 (Id)
00:51:33: OSPF: Send DBD to 192.168.31.33 on FastEthernet0/0 seq
        0x21CF opt 0x2 flag 0x7 len 32
00:51:33: OSPF: Send with youngest Key 1
00:51:33: OSPF: Remember old DR 192.168.31.22 (id)
00:51:33: OSPF: End of hello processing
```

Step 4

At this point, SanJose1 should have assumed the role of BDR. Bring SanJose3 back online, and observe the new election process.

4. SanJose3 will assume its former role as DR. Who is elected BDR? Why?

_____

SanJose1 remains the BDR even though SanJose2 has the higher router ID.

Step 5

You can manipulate which router becomes the DR using two methods. You could change the router's router ID to a higher number, but that could confuse your loopback addressing system and affect elections on other interfaces. The same router ID is used for every network that a router is a member of. For example, if an OSPF router has an exceptionally high router ID, it could win the election on every multiaccess interface and, as a result, do triple or quadruple duty as a DR.

Instead of reconfiguring router IDs, you manipulate the election by configuring OSPF priority values. Because priorities are an interface-specific value, they provide finer control of your OSPF internetwork by allowing a router to be the DR in one network and a DRother in another. Priority values are the first consideration in the DR election; highest priority wins. Values can range from 0-255; a value of 0 indicates that the interface will not participate in an election. Use the **show ip ospf interface** command to examine the current priority values of the three routers' Ethernet interfaces:

```
SanJose1#show ip ospf interface
FastEthernet0/0 is up, line protocol is up
  Internet Address 192.168.1.1/24, Area 0
  Process ID 1, Router ID 192.168.31.11, Network Type BROADCAST,
      Cost: 1
  Transmit Delay is 1 sec, State BDR, Priority 1
  Designated Router (ID) 192.168.31.33, Interface address
      192.168.1.3
  Backup Designated router (ID) 192.168.31.11, Interface address
      192.168.1.1
  Timer intervals configured, Hello 5, Dead 20, Wait 20,
      Retransmit 5
    Hello due in 00:00:03
  Index 1/1, flood queue length 0
  Next 0x0(0)/0x0(0)
```

```
Last flood scan length is 1, maximum is 2
Last flood scan time is 0 msec, maximum is 0 msec
Neighbor Count is 2, Adjacent neighbor count is 2
  Adjacent with neighbor 192.168.31.33   (Designated Router)
  Adjacent with neighbor 192.168.31.22
Suppress hello for 0 neighbor(s)
Message digest authentication enabled
  Youngest key id is 1
```

5. What is the priority value of these interfaces?

_____

The default priority is 1. Because all have equal priority, router ID is used to determine the DR and BDR.

Modify the priority values so that SanJose1 will become the DR and SanJose2 will become the BDR, regardless of their router ID. Use the following commands:

```
SanJose1(config)#interface fastethernet 0/0
SanJose1(config-if)#ip ospf priority 200

SanJose2(config)#interface fastethernet 0/0
SanJose2(config-if)#ip ospf priority 100
```

In order to reset the election process, you must write each router's configuration to NVRAM and reload SanJose1, SanJose2, and SanJose3. You can issue the following commands at each router:

```
SanJose1#copy running-config startup-config
SanJose1#reload
```

When the routers finish reloading, try to observe the OSPF election on SanJose1 by using the **debug ip ospf adj** command. You can also verify your configuration by issuing the **show ip ospf interface** command at both SanJose1 and SanJose2.

```
SanJose1#debug ip ospf adj
00:01:20: OSPF: Rcv hello from 192.168.31.22 area 0 from
        FastEthernet0/0 192.168.1.2
00:01:20: OSPF: Neighbor change Event on interface FastEthernet0/0
00:01:20: OSPF: DR/BDR election on FastEthernet0/0
00:01:20: OSPF: Elect BDR 192.168.31.22
00:01:20: OSPF: Elect DR 192.168.31.11
00:01:20:          DR: 192.168.31.11 (Id)    BDR: 192.168.31.22 (Id)
00:01:20: OSPF: End of hello processing

SanJose2#show ip ospf interface
FastEthernet0/0 is up, line protocol is up
  Internet Address 192.168.1.2/24, Area 0
  Process ID 1, Router ID 192.168.31.22, Network Type BROADCAST,
      Cost: 1
  Transmit Delay is 1 sec, State BDR, Priority 100
  Designated Router (ID) 192.168.31.11, Interface address
      192.168.1.1
  Backup Designated router (ID) 192.168.31.22, Interface address
      192.168.1.2
  Timer intervals configured, Hello 5, Dead 20, Wait 20,
```

```
        Retransmit 5
      Hello due in 00:00:03
   Index 1/1, flood queue length 0
   Next 0x0(0)/0x0(0)
   Last flood scan length is 1, maximum is 1
   Last flood scan time is 0 msec, maximum is 0 msec
   Neighbor Count is 2, Adjacent neighbor count is 2
     Adjacent with neighbor 192.168.31.33
     Adjacent with neighbor 192.168.31.11   (Designated Router)
   Suppress hello for 0 neighbor(s)
   Message digest authentication enabled
     Youngest key id is 1
```

After the election is complete, verify that SanJose1 and SanJose2 have assumed the correct roles by using the **show ip ospf neighbor detail** command. Troubleshoot, if necessary.

```
SanJose3#show ip ospf neighbor detail
Neighbor 192.168.31.22, interface address 192.168.1.2
   In the area 0 via interface FastEthernet0/0
   Neighbor priority is 100, State is FULL, 6 state changes
   DR is 192.168.1.1 BDR is 192.168.1.2
   Options 2
   Dead timer due in 00:00:17
   Index 2/2, retransmission queue length 0, number of
     retransmission 0
   First 0x0(0)/0x0(0) Next 0x0(0)/0x0(0)
   Last retransmission scan length is 0, maximum is 0
   Last retransmission scan time is 0 msec, maximum is 0 msec
Neighbor 192.168.31.11, interface address 192.168.1.1
   In the area 0 via interface FastEthernet0/0
   Neighbor priority is 200, State is FULL, 6 state changes
   DR is 192.168.1.1 BDR is 192.168.1.2
   Options 2
   Dead timer due in 00:00:19
   Index 1/1, retransmission queue length 0, number of
     retransmission 2
   First 0x0(0)/0x0(0) Next 0x0(0)/0x0(0)
   Last retransmission scan length is 1, maximum is 1
   Last retransmission scan time is 0 msec, maximum is 0 msec
```

Note that the order in which routers join an area can have the most significant effect on which routers are elected as DR and BDR. An election is necessary only when a DR or BDR does not exist in the network. As a router starts its OSPF process, it checks the network for an active DR and BDR. If they exist, the new router becomes a DRother, regardless of its priority or router ID. Remember, the roles of DR and BDR were created for efficiency; "new" routers in the network should not force an election when adjacencies are already optimized. However, there is an exception. A known bug in some IOS versions allows a "new" router with higher election credentials to force an election and assume the role of DR.

Lab 4-3: Configuring Point-to-Multipoint OSPF Over Frame Relay

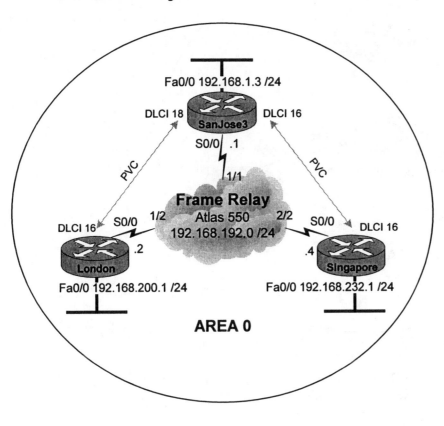

or

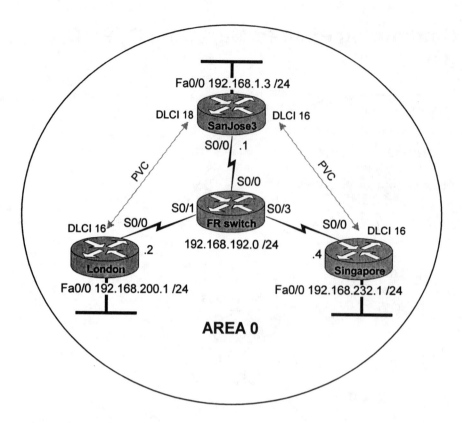

Objective

In this lab, configure OSPF as a point-to-multipoint network type so that it operates efficiently over a hub-and-spoke Frame Relay topology.

Scenario

International Travel Agency has just connected two regional headquarters to San Jose using Frame Relay in a hub-and-spoke topology. You are asked to configure OSPF routing over this type of network, which is known for introducing complications into OSPF adjacency relationships. To avoid these complications, you must manually override the Non-Broadcast Multi-Access (NBMA) OSPF network type and configure OSPF to run as a point-to-multipoint network. In this environment, no DR or BDR is elected.

Step 1

Cable the network according to the diagram. (*Note:* This lab requires another router or device to act as a Frame Relay switch.) The first diagram assumes that you will use an Adtran Atlas 550, which is preconfigured. The second diagram assumes that you will configure a router with at least three serial interfaces as a Frame Relay switch. See the configuration at the end of this lab for an example of how to configure a router as a Frame Relay switch. If desired, you can copy the configuration to a 2600 router for use in this lab.

Configure each router's FastEthernet interface as shown, but leave the serial interfaces and OSPF routing unconfigured for now. Assign loopback interfaces to each router at your discretion (be sure they are unique within your network).

Until you configure Frame Relay, you will not be able to use ping to test connectivity.

Step 2

SanJose3 acts as the hub in this hub-and-spoke network. It reaches London and Singapore via two separate PVCs. Configure Frame Relay on SanJose3's serial interface as shown here:

```
SanJose3(config)#interface serial 0/0
SanJose3(config-if)#encapsulation frame-relay ietf
SanJose3(config-if)#ip address 192.168.192.1 255.255.255.0
SanJose3(config-if)#no shutdown
SanJose3(config-if)#frame-relay map ip 192.168.192.2 18 broadcast
SanJose3(config-if)#frame-relay map ip 192.168.192.4 16 broadcast
SanJose3(config-if)#ip ospf network point-to-multipoint
```

Note that this configuration includes **frame-relay map** commands, which are typically used with Frame Relay subinterfaces. These commands are needed here so that you can configure Frame Relay to handle broadcast traffic with the **broadcast** keyword. Without this configuration, OSPF multicast traffic will not be forwarded correctly over this Frame Relay topology.

Configure London's serial interface; use IETF encapsulation:

```
London(config)#interface serial 0/0
London(config-if)#encapsulation frame-relay ietf
London(config-if)#ip address 192.168.192.2 255.255.255.0
London(config-if)#no shutdown
London(config-if)#frame-relay map ip 192.168.192.1 17 broadcast
London(config-if)#frame-relay map ip 192.168.192.4 17 broadcast
London(config-if)#ip ospf network point-to-multipoint
```

Finally, configure Singapore's serial interface:

```
Singapore(config)#interface serial 0/0
Singapore(config-if)#encapsulation frame-relay IETF
Singapore(config-if)#ip address 192.168.192.4 255.255.255.0
Singapore(config-if)#no shutdown
Singapore(config-if)#frame-relay map ip 192.168.192.1 17 broadcast
Singapore(config-if)#frame-relay map ip 192.168.192.2 17 broadcast
Singapore(config-if)#ip ospf network point-to-multipoint
```

Verify Frame Relay operation with a **ping** from each router to the other two. Use **show frame-relay pvc** and **show frame-relay map** to troubleshoot connectivity problems. Rebooting the Frame Relay switch might also solve connectivity issues.

```
SanJose3#show frame-relay pvc

PVC Statistics for interface Serial0/0 (Frame Relay DTE)
```

```
              Active     Inactive     Deleted      Static
Local          2            0            0            0
Switched       0            0            0            0
Unused         0            0            0            0

DLCI = 17, DLCI USAGE = LOCAL, PVC STATUS = ACTIVE, INTERFACE =
       Serial0/0

   input pkts 91          output pkts 76          in bytes 13322
   out bytes 14796        dropped pkts 10         in FECN pkts 0
   in BECN pkts 0         out FECN pkts 0         out BECN pkts 0
   in DE pkts 0           out DE pkts 0
   out bcast pkts 50       out bcast bytes 9808
   pvc create time 00:38:04, last time pvc status changed 00:01:18

DLCI = 18, DLCI USAGE = LOCAL, PVC STATUS = ACTIVE, INTERFACE =
       Serial0/0

   input pkts 61          output pkts 57          in bytes 10786
   out bytes 14076        dropped pkts 4          in FECN pkts 0
   in BECN pkts 0         out FECN pkts 0         out BECN pkts 0
   in DE pkts 0           out DE pkts 0
   out bcast pkts 30       out bcast bytes 8940
   pvc create time 00:48:17, last time pvc status changed 00:03:31


SanJose3#show frame-relay map
Serial0/0 (up): ip 192.168.192.2 dlci 18(0x12,0x420), static,
               broadcast,
               IETF, status defined, active
Serial0/0 (up): ip 192.168.192.4 dlci 17(0x11,0x410), static,
               broadcast,
               IETF, status defined, active
```

Step 3

Configure OSPF to run over this point-to-multipoint network. Issue the following commands at the appropriate router:

```
London(config)#router ospf 1
London(config-router)#network 192.168.200.0 0.0.0.255 area 0
London(config-router)#network 192.168.192.0 0.0.0.255 area 0

SanJose3(config)#router ospf 1
SanJose3(config-router)#network 192.168.1.0 0.0.0.255 area 0
SanJose3(config-router)#network 192.168.192 0.0.0.255 area 0

Singapore(config)#router ospf 1
Singapore(config-router)#network 192.168.232.0 0.0.0.255 area 0
Singapore(config-router)#network 192.168.192.0 0.0.0.255 area 0
```

Verify your OSPF configuration by issuing the **show ip route** command at each of the routers:

```
London#show ip route

Gateway of last resort is not set

     192.168.192.0/24 is variably subnetted, 3 subnets, 2 masks
C       192.168.192.0/24 is directly connected, Serial0/0
```

```
O          192.168.192.1/32 [110/64] via 192.168.192.1, 00:06:49,
           Serial0/0
192.168.192.4/32 [110/128] via 192.168.192.1, 00:06:49,
Serial0/0
C     192.168.200.0/24 is directly connected, FastEthernet0/0
O     192.168.232.0/24 [110/129] via 192.168.192.1, 00:06:49,
           Serial0/0
      192.168.204.0/32 is subnetted, 1 subnets
C          192.168.204.1 is directly connected, Loopback0
O     192.168.1.0/24 [110/65] via 192.168.192.1, 00:06:50,
           Serial0/0
```

If each router has a complete table, including routes to 192.168.1.0 /24, 192.168.200.0 /24, and 192.168.232.0 /24, you have successfully configured OSPF to operate over Frame Relay.

Test these routes by pinging the FastEthernet interfaces of each router from London's console.

Finally, issue the **show ip ospf neighbor detail** command at any router's console:

```
SanJose3#show ip ospf neighbor

Neighbor ID     Pri   State      Dead Time   Address         Interface
192.168.200.1    1    FULL/  -   00:01:35    192.168.192.2   Serial0/0
192.168.232.1    1    FULL/  -   00:01:51    192.168.192.4   Serial0/0
```

```
      SanJose3#show ip ospf neighbor detail
       Neighbor 192.168.200.1, interface address 192.168.192.2
          In the area 0 via interface Serial0/0
          Neighbor priority is 1, State is FULL, 6 state changes
          DR is 0.0.0.0 BDR is 0.0.0.0
          Options 2
          Dead timer due in 00:01:41
          Index 2/2, retransmission queue length 0, number of
             retransmission 1
          First 0x0(0)/0x0(0) Next 0x0(0)/0x0(0)
          Last retransmission scan length is 1, maximum is 1
          Last retransmission scan time is 0 msec, maximum is 0 msec
       Neighbor 192.168.232.1, interface address 192.168.192.4
          In the area 0 via interface Serial0/0
          Neighbor priority is 1, State is FULL, 6 state changes
          DR is 0.0.0.0 BDR is 0.0.0.0
          Options 2
          Dead timer due in 00:01:56
          Index 1/1, retransmission queue length 0, number of
             retransmission 1
          First 0x0(0)/0x0(0) Next 0x0(0)/0x0(0)
          Last retransmission scan length is 1, maximum is 1
          Last retransmission scan time is 0 msec, maximum is 0 msec
```

1. Is there a DR for this network? Why or why not?

_____

_____

There is no DR. Point-to-multipoint configuration creates a logical multiaccess network over physical point-to-point links. Because each router has only one physical neighbor, only one adjacency can be formed. No efficiency would be realized by electing a DR.

Router as Frame Relay Switch Configuration

The following example can be used to configure a router as the Frame Relay switch.

```
Frame-Switch#show run
version 12.0
service timestamps debug uptime
service timestamps log uptime
no service password-encryption
!
hostname Frame-Switch
!
ip subnet-zero
no ip domain-lookup
!
ip audit notify log
ip audit po max-events 100
frame-relay switching
!
process-max-time 200
!
interface Serial0/0
 no ip address
 no ip directed-broadcast
 encapsulation frame-relay
 clockrate 56000
 cdp enable
 frame-relay intf-type dce
 frame-relay route 17 interface Serial0/2 16
 frame-relay route 18 interface Serial0/1 16
!
interface Serial0/1
 no ip address
 no ip directed-broadcast
 encapsulation frame-relay
 clockrate 56000
 cdp enable
 frame-relay intf-type dce
 frame-relay route 16 interface Serial0/0 18
!
interface Serial0/2
 no ip address
 no ip directed-broadcast
 encapsulation frame-relay
 clockrate 56000
 cdp enable
 frame-relay intf-type dce
 frame-relay route 16 interface Serial0/0 17
!
```

```
interface Serial0/3
 no ip address
 no ip directed-broadcast
 shutdown
!
ip classless
no ip http server
!
line con 0
 password cisco
 login
 transport input none
line aux 0
line vty 0 4
 password cisco
 login
!
no scheduler allocate
end
```

Lab 5-1: Multiarea OSPF

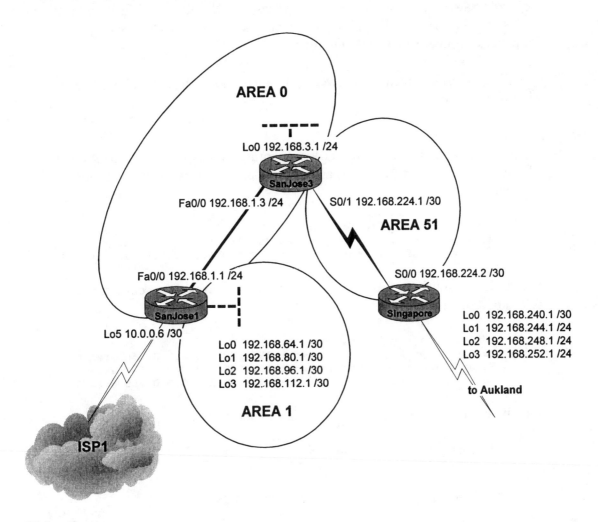

Objective

In this lab, you configure multiarea OSPF operation, interarea summarization, external route summarization, and default routing.

Scenario

International Travel Agency (ITA) maintains a complex OSPF environment. Your manager asks you to optimize OSPF routing. You need to design and configure multiarea OSPF on the key routers connecting Asian regional headquarters to San Jose corporate headquarters and its local sites.

Step 1

Build and configure the network according to the diagram, but do not configure a routing protocol yet. *Note:* This lab requires the use of subnet 0. You can ignore the ISP1 cloud for now.

Configure each router with the loopback address indicated in the diagram. Be sure to configure SanJose1 and Singapore with additional loopbacks (Lo0, Lo1, Lo2, Lo3). On SanJose1, these loopback interfaces simulate the serial links to local San Jose sites: Westasman, Baypointe, Vista, and Eastasman. On Singapore, the loopbacks simulate Auckland networks.

Use **ping** to test connectivity between all interfaces. Each router should be able to ping its serial link partner.

Step 2

Configure multiarea OSPF. On SanJose1, configure FastEthernet 0/0 as a member of Area 0 and all other interfaces as members of Area 1 by using the following commands:

```
SanJose1(config)#router ospf 1
SanJose1(config-router)#network 192.168.1.0 0.0.0.255 area 0
SanJose1(config-router)#network 192.168.64.0 0.0.63.255 area 1
```

On SanJose3, configure E0 and Lo0 as members of Area 0, but configure Serial 0/0 as part of Area 51:

```
SanJose3(config)#router ospf 1
SanJose3(config-router)#network 192.168.1.0 0.0.0.255 area 0
SanJose3(config-router)#network 192.168.224.0 0.0.0.3 area 51
SanJose3(config-router)#network 192.168.3.0 0.0.0.255 area 0
```

Finally, on Singapore, configure Serial 0/0 to belong to Area 51:

```
Singapore(config)#router ospf 1
Singapore(config-router)#network 192.168.224.0 0.0.0.3 area 51
```

Issue the **show ip ospf** command on all three routers:

```
SanJose3#show ip ospf
 Routing Process "ospf 1" with ID 192.168.3.1
 Supports only single TOS(TOS0) routes
 It is an area border router
 SPF schedule delay 5 secs, Hold time between two SPFs 10 secs
 Minimum LSA interval 5 secs. Minimum LSA arrival 1 secs
 Number of external LSA 0. Checksum Sum 0x0
 Number of DCbitless external LSA 0
 Number of DoNotAge external LSA 0
 Number of areas in this router is 2. 2 normal 0 stub 0 nssa
 External flood list length 0
    Area BACKBONE(0)
        Number of interfaces in this area is 2
        Area has no authentication
        SPF algorithm executed 6 times
        Area ranges are
        Number of LSA 8. Checksum Sum 0x42B0C
        Number of DCbitless LSA 0
        Number of indication LSA 0
        Number of DoNotAge LSA 0
        Flood list length 0
    Area 51
```

```
Number of interfaces in this area is 1
Area has no authentication
SPF algorithm executed 4 times
Area ranges are
Number of LSA 8. Checksum Sum 0x59B4F
Number of DCbitless LSA 0
Number of indication LSA 0
Number of DoNotAge LSA 0
Flood list length 0
```

1. According to the output of the **show ip ospf** command, which of these routers is an ABR?

Area Border Routers connect one or more adjacent OSPF areas to the backbone area.

2. Are there any ASBRs?

Autonomous System Border Routers connect external (non-OSPF) networks to the OSPF internetwork.

Issue the **show ip ospf neighbor detail** command on SanJose3:

```
SanJose3#show ip ospf neighbor detail
Neighbor 192.168.112.1, interface address 192.168.1.1
    In the area 0 via interface FastEthernet0/0
    Neighbor priority is 1, State is FULL, 6 state changes
    DR is 192.168.1.1 BDR is 192.168.1.3
    Options 2
    Dead timer due in 00:00:33
    Index 1/1, retransmission queue length 0, number of
      retransmission 2
    First 0x0(0)/0x0(0) Next 0x0(0)/0x0(0)
    Last retransmission scan length is 1, maximum is 1
    Last retransmission scan time is 0 msec, maximum is 0 msec
Neighbor 192.168.252.1, interface address 192.168.224.2
    In the area 51 via interface Serial0/0
    Neighbor priority is 1, State is FULL, 6 state changes
    DR is 0.0.0.0 BDR is 0.0.0.0
    Options 2
    Dead timer due in 00:00:32
    Index 1/2, retransmission queue length 0, number of
      retransmission 1
    First 0x0(0)/0x0(0) Next 0x0(0)/0x0(0)
    Last retransmission scan length is 1, maximum is 1
    Last retransmission scan time is 0 msec, maximum is 0 msec
```

3. Is a designated router on the 192.168.1.0/24 network? Why or why not?

---

4. Is a designated router on the 192.168.224.0/30 network? Why or why not?

_____

_____

These are different types of OSPF networks. The Ethernet core network is designated as BROADCAST, and the WAN link between SanJose3 and Singapore is designated POINT_TO_POINT. On a point-to-point link, there's no need to elect a DR to reduce the number of adjacencies, because only two routers exist in the network. The Ethernet segment has only two routers, but a DR and BDR are elected because other routers (neighbors) could join the area.

Step 3

Check each router's routing table. You should see OSPF intra-area routes, which are denoted by an O. You should also see routes denoted by an IA.

```
Singapore#show ip route
Codes: C - connected, S - static, I - IGRP, R - RIP, M - mobile,
       B - BGP
       D - EIGRP, EX - EIGRP external, O - OSPF, IA - OSPF
       inter area
       N1 - OSPF NSSA external type 1, N2 - OSPF NSSA external
       type 2
       E1 - OSPF external type 1, E2 - OSPF external type 2,
       E - EGP
       i - IS-IS, L1 - IS-IS level-1, L2 - IS-IS level-2, ia -
       IS-IS inter area
       * - candidate default, U - per-user static route, o - ODR
       P - periodic downloaded static route

Gateway of last resort is not set

     192.168.224.0/30 is subnetted, 1 subnets
C       192.168.224.0 is directly connected, Serial0/0
     192.168.240.0/30 is subnetted, 1 subnets
C       192.168.240.0 is directly connected, Loopback0
     192.168.244.0/30 is subnetted, 1 subnets
C       192.168.244.0 is directly connected, Loopback1
     192.168.64.0/32 is subnetted, 1 subnets
O IA    192.168.64.1 [110/66] via 192.168.224.1, 00:27:14,
          Serial0/0
     192.168.80.0/32 is subnetted, 1 subnets
O IA    192.168.80.1 [110/66] via 192.168.224.1, 00:27:14,
          Serial0/0
     192.168.96.0/32 is subnetted, 1 subnets
O IA    192.168.96.1 [110/66] via 192.168.224.1, 00:27:15,
          Serial0/0
     192.168.248.0/30 is subnetted, 1 subnets
C       192.168.248.0 is directly connected, Loopback2
     192.168.112.0/32 is subnetted, 1 subnets
O IA    192.168.112.1 [110/66] via 192.168.224.1, 00:27:16,
          Serial0/0
O IA 192.168.1.0/24 [110/65] via 192.168.224.1, 00:27:16,
          Serial0/0
     192.168.252.0/30 is subnetted, 1 subnets
C       192.168.252.0 is directly connected, Loopback3
     192.168.3.0/32 is subnetted, 1 subnets
O IA    192.168.3.1 [110/65] via 192.168.224.1, 00:27:16,
          Serial0/0
```

5. What does IA stand for?

_____

Check the codes listed with the routing table. Interarea routes point to networks in separate areas within the same OSPF autonomous system.
Verify that your routing tables are complete. Notice that SanJose1's loopback interfaces appear in the other router's tables with a 32-bit mask. Any route with a 32-bit mask is called a *host route*, because it is a route to a host, not to a network. OSPF does not advertise loopback interfaces as if they were connected to a network.

6. How many host routes are in Singapore's table?

_____

There should be a host route for every remote loopback advertised through OSPF.

Verify connectivity. From Singapore, ping SanJose3's Lo0 interface (192.168.3.1) and SanJose1's Lo2 interface (192.168.96.1).

Step 4

To reduce routing table entries, you decide to implement interarea route summarization throughout the internetwork. You must start by configuring SanJose1 to summarize Area 1's networks and advertise this summary route to Area 0.

On SanJose1, enter the following commands to perform interarea summarization:

```
SanJose1(config)#router ospf 1
SanJose1(config-router)#area 1 range 192.168.64.0 255.255.192.0
```

When you finish configuring the summary address, check the routing tables of SanJose3 and Singapore. If the expected changes do not occur, save and reload the routers.

```
Singapore#show ip route

     192.168.224.0/30 is subnetted, 1 subnets
C       192.168.224.0 is directly connected, Serial0/0
     192.168.240.0/30 is subnetted, 1 subnets
C       192.168.240.0 is directly connected, Loopback0
     192.168.244.0/30 is subnetted, 1 subnets
C       192.168.244.0 is directly connected, Loopback1
     192.168.248.0/30 is subnetted, 1 subnets
C       192.168.248.0 is directly connected, Loopback2
O IA 192.168.1.0/24 [110/65] via 192.168.224.1, 00:35:10,
        Serial0/0
     192.168.252.0/30 is subnetted, 1 subnets
C       192.168.252.0 is directly connected, Loopback3
     192.168.3.0/32 is subnetted, 1 subnets
O IA    192.168.3.1 [110/65] via 192.168.224.1, 00:35:11,
        Serial0/0
O IA 192.168.64.0/18 [110/66] via 192.168.224.1, 00:02:17,
        Serial0/0
```

7. What happened to the host routes?

_____

_____

8. How many host routes does Singapore have?

_____

9. Singapore should still be able to ping 192.168.96.1. Why?

_____

10. What network is Singapore sending ICMP requests to?

_____

Singapore should have only one host route of 192.168.3.1/32 from SanJose3 Lo0. A host route points to one host. A network route points to multiple hosts in one broadcast domain. A summarized route points to a numerically contiguous series of networks.

Step 5

You must configure Singapore to redistribute external routes from Auckland into your OSPF autonomous system. For the purposes of this lab, you simulate the Auckland connection by configuring a static route in Singapore to the Auckland LAN (192.168.248.0/24). Use the following commands:

```
Singapore(config)#ip route 192.168.248.0 255.255.255.0 null0
Singapore(config)#router ospf 1
Singapore(config-router)#redistribute static
```

Because the route to 192.168.248.0/24 is imaginary, null0 is used as the exit interface. The **redistribute** command imports the static route into OSPF. Routes originated from anything but OSPF are considered external to the OSPF database. By default, when Singapore redistributes into Area 51, it creates and advertises Type 2 (E2) external routes using Type 5 LSAs.

Issue the **show ip ospf** command on Singapore.

11. According to the output of this command, what type of OSPF router is Singapore?

_____

```
Singapore#show ip ospf
  Routing Process "ospf 1" with ID 192.168.252.1
  Supports only single TOS(TOS0) routes
  It is an autonomous system boundary router
  Redistributing External Routes from,
     static
  SPF schedule delay 5 secs, Hold time between two SPFs 10 secs
  Minimum LSA interval 5 secs. Minimum LSA arrival 1 secs
  Number of external LSA 1. Checksum Sum 0x8650
  Number of DCbitless external LSA 0
  Number of DoNotAge external LSA 0
```

```
Number of areas in this router is 1. 1 normal 0 stub 0 nssa
External flood list length 0
    Area 51
        Number of interfaces in this area is 1
        Area has no authentication
        SPF algorithm executed 4 times
        Area ranges are
        Number of LSA 5. Checksum Sum 0x3A27A
        Number of DCbitless LSA 0
        Number of indication LSA 0
        Number of DoNotAge LSA 0
        Flood list length 0
```

Recall that ASBRs connect external networks to the OSPF autonomous system.

Now check the routing table of SanJose1. It should have an E2 route to 192.168.248.0/24.

```
SanJose1#show ip route

        192.168.224.0/30 is subnetted, 1 subnets
O IA    192.168.224.0 [110/782] via 192.168.1.3, 00:04:39,
        FastEthernet0/0
        192.168.64.0/30 is subnetted, 1 subnets
C       192.168.64.0 is directly connected, Loopback0
        192.168.80.0/30 is subnetted, 1 subnets
C       192.168.80.0 is directly connected, Loopback1
        192.168.96.0/30 is subnetted, 1 subnets
C       192.168.96.0 is directly connected, Loopback2
O E2    192.168.248.0/24 [110/20] via 192.168.1.3, 00:03:57,
        FastEthernet0/0
        192.168.112.0/30 is subnetted, 1 subnets
C       192.168.112.0 is directly connected, Loopback3
C       192.168.1.0/24 is directly connected, FastEthernet0/0
        192.168.3.0/32 is subnetted, 1 subnets
O       192.168.3.1 [110/2] via 192.168.1.3, 00:08:08,
        FastEthernet0/0
```

12. What is the metric (OSPF cost) of this route?

_____

Check SanJose1's routing table; it too should have the external route.

13. What is the metric of SanJose3's route to 192.168.248.0/24?

_____

You should see that SanJose1 and SanJose3 have the same cost. This might be surprising, because SanJose1 has an additional network to traverse.

A second link to the external network is about to come online. If your network is designed so that OSPF routers can have multiple external routes to the same destination, you should consider using Type 1 (E1) external routes. Type 2 (E2) external routes have static metrics throughout your OSPF autonomous system (AS). Type 1 routes consider metrics internal and external to your AS for accurate route selection when multiple external routes exist. You decide that Singapore should advertise external routes as Type 1 (E1). To configure Type 1, use the following commands on Singapore:

```
Singapore(config)#router ospf 1
Singapore(config-router)#redistribute static metric-type 1
```

After you reconfigure Singapore, check SanJose3's table again. SanJose3's route to 192.168.248.0/24 should now be FastEthernet 0/1.

14. What is the metric of this route?

_____

Check SanJose1's route to 192.168.248.0/24.

15. What is the metric of Singapore's route?

_____

Typically, the cost of a route increases with every hop. Type2 (E2) routes ignore internal OSPF metrics. Type1 (E1) routes accumulate costs while being propagated through the OSPF AS. With one egress point for your AS, Type2 (E2) routes might be adequate.

Step 6

Over time, you noticed that, as the Auckland office grows, many more Type 1 (FastEthernet 0/1) networks are propagated through your internetwork. You want to optimize your internetwork by reducing the routing table size. You choose to implement Classless Interdomain Routing (CIDR) to advertise all Auckland networks with one route. Create routes to these Auckland networks with three more static routes:

```
Singapore(config)#ip route 192.168.240.0 255.255.255.252 null0
Singapore(config)#ip route 192.168.244.0 255.255.255.0 null0
Singapore(config)#ip route 192.168.252.0 255.255.255.0 null0
```

Configure Singapore to advertise all Auckland networks with a summary route:

```
Singapore(config)#router ospf 1
Singapore(config-router)#summary-address 192.168.240.0
    255.255.240.0
```

After you configure the summary, check the routing tables on SanJose1 and SanJose3. Both routers should receive and install the supernet route, 192.168.240.0/20. (*Note:* On routers with very large routing tables, you can issue the command **show ip route supernet** to view only aggregate routes.)

```
SanJose3#show ip route
     192.168.224.0/30 is subnetted, 1 subnets
C       192.168.224.0 is directly connected, Serial0/0
C    192.168.1.0/24 is directly connected, FastEthernet0/0
C    192.168.3.0/24 is directly connected, Loopback0
O*E2 0.0.0.0/0 [110/1] via 192.168.1.1, 00:00:44, FastEthernet0/0
```

```
O E2 192.168.240.0/20 [110/20] via 192.168.224.2, 00:00:44,
        Serial0/0
O IA 192.168.64.0/18 [110/2] via 192.168.1.1, 00:00:44,
        FastEthernet0/0

SanJose1#show ip route supernet
O E2 192.168.240.0/20 [110/20] via 192.168.1.3, 00:01:19,
        FastEthernet0/0
```

16. Is 192.168.248.0/24 still in SanJose1 or SanJose3's routing table?

You should not see it. Network 192.168.248.0/24 is included in the range 192.168.240.0/20.

You negotiated Internet connectivity with your service provider. You need to connect to ISP1 through SanJose1. The link isn't active yet, but you decide to configure OSPF in advance. Simulate the link you will have with a loopback interface:

```
SanJose1(config)#interface lo5
SanJose1(config-if)#ip address 10.0.0.6 255.255.255.255
```

Use the following commands to create and advertise a default route on SanJose1:

```
SanJose1(config)#router ospf 1
SanJose1(config-router)#default-information originate always
```

The **always** keyword instructs OSPF to advertise the default route whether or not the router has one. Check the routing tables on SanJose3 and Singapore. Both should now have a default route (0.0.0.0/0).

```
SanJose3#show ip route

     192.168.224.0/30 is subnetted, 1 subnets
C       192.168.224.0 is directly connected, Serial0/0
C    192.168.1.0/24 is directly connected, FastEthernet0/0
C    192.168.3.0/24 is directly connected, Loopback0
O*E2 0.0.0.0/0 [110/1] via 192.168.1.1, 00:00:44, FastEthernet0/0
O E2 192.168.240.0/20 [110/20] via 192.168.224.2, 00:00:44,
        Serial0/0
O IA 192.168.64.0/18 [110/2] via 192.168.1.1, 00:00:44,
        FastEthernet0/0
```

17. What type of OSPF route is the default?

---

18. What is the metric of this route on SanJose3?

---

19. What is the metric of this route on Singapore?

The default route is considered External Type2 (E2). The default cost of 1 will be retained throughout the autonomous system.

To test the default route configuration, create a loopback interface on SanJose1 to simulate the serial interface that will connect to ISP1:

```
SanJose1(config)#interface lo5
SanJose1(config-if)#ip address 10.0.0.6 255.255.255.252
```

Verify that default routing is working by asking Singapore to ping a host that is not represented in its routing table. From Singapore, ping 10.0.0.6. If the default route is working, Singapore should receive replies. Troubleshoot, if necessary.

Lab 5-2: Configuring a Stub Area and a Totally Stubby Area

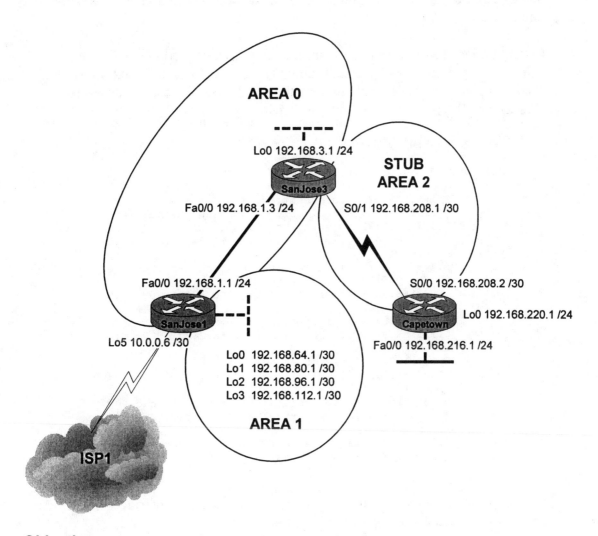

Objective

In this lab, you configure an OSPF stub area and a totally stubby area.

Scenario

You receive a request from technical support in Capetown to upgrade their router. They suspect that the router is not keeping up with the growth of your OSPF internetwork. You run some diagnostics and discover that the router could benefit from more memory due to the large routing table. The router could also use a faster processor because of frequent Shortest Path First calculations. You decide instead to create a smaller and more stable routing table using a stub or totally stubby area configuration.

Step 1

Build and configure the network according to the diagram. Configure multiarea OSPF according to the diagram (do not configure a stub area yet). *Note:* This lab requires the use of subnet 0. You can ignore the loopback Lo5 on SanJose1 for now.

Configure each router with the loopback address as indicated in the diagram. Be sure to configure SanJose1 with additional loopbacks (Lo0, Lo1, Lo2, Lo3). These loopback interfaces will simulate the serial links to local San Jose sites: Westasman, Baypointe, Vista, and Eastasman.

```
CapeTown#show ip route

Gateway of last resort is not set

     192.168.208.0/30 is subnetted, 1 subnets
C        192.168.208.0 is directly connected, Serial0/0
     192.168.64.0/32 is subnetted, 1 subnets
O IA    192.168.64.1 [110/66] via 192.168.208.1, 00:20:04,
         Serial0/0
C    192.168.216.0/24 is directly connected, FastEthernet0/0
     192.168.80.0/32 is subnetted, 1 subnets
O IA    192.168.80.1 [110/66] via 192.168.208.1, 00:20:04,
         Serial0/0
     192.168.96.0/32 is subnetted, 1 subnets
O IA    192.168.96.1 [110/66] via 192.168.208.1, 00:20:04,
         Serial0/0
     192.168.112.0/32 is subnetted, 1 subnets
O IA    192.168.112.1 [110/66] via 192.168.208.1, 00:20:05,
         Serial0/0
C    192.168.220.0/24 is directly connected, Loopback0
O IA 192.168.1.0/24 [110/65] via 192.168.208.1, 00:20:05,
         Serial0/0
     192.168.3.0/32 is subnetted, 1 subnets
O IA    192.168.3.1 [110/65] via 192.168.208.1, 00:20:07,
         Serial0/0
```

Use **ping** and **show ip route** to test connectivity between all interfaces. Each router should be able to ping all network interfaces.

Step 2

Configure SanJose1 to redistribute an external route into the OSPF domain:

```
SanJose1(config)#ip route 10.0.0.0 255.0.0.0 null0
SanJose1(config)#router ospf 1
SanJose1(config-router)#redistribute static
```

Also, create a loopback interface to simulate the serial interface connecting to ISP1:

```
SanJose1(config)#interface lo5
SanJose1(config-if)#ip address 10.0.0.6 255.255.255.252
```

Check the routing tables of all three routers; they should be complete.

```
CapeTown#show ip route

Gateway of last resort is not set

     192.168.208.0/30 is subnetted, 1 subnets
C       192.168.208.0 is directly connected, Serial0/0
     192.168.64.0/32 is subnetted, 1 subnets
O IA    192.168.64.1 [110/66] via 192.168.208.1, 00:07:32,
        Serial0/0
C    192.168.216.0/24 is directly connected, FastEthernet0/0
     192.168.80.0/32 is subnetted, 1 subnets
O IA    192.168.80.1 [110/66] via 192.168.208.1, 00:07:32,
        Serial0/0
O E2 10.0.0.0/8 [110/20] via 192.168.208.1, 00:00:35, Serial0/0
     192.168.96.0/32 is subnetted, 1 subnets
O IA    192.168.96.1 [110/66] via 192.168.208.1, 00:07:32,
        Serial0/0
     192.168.112.0/32 is subnetted, 1 subnets
O IA    192.168.112.1 [110/66] via 192.168.208.1, 00:07:32,
        Serial0/0
C    192.168.220.0/24 is directly connected, Loopback0
O IA 192.168.1.0/24 [110/65] via 192.168.208.1, 00:07:34,
        Serial0/0
     192.168.3.0/32 is subnetted, 1 subnets
O IA    192.168.3.1 [110/65] via 192.168.208.1, 00:07:34,
        Serial0/0
```

SanJose3 and Capetown should also have a Type 2 external route to 10.0.0.0/8. They will not have a specific route to the loopback (10.0.0.4/30). That network has not explicitly been advertised by any means.

Step 3

Capetown has several interarea (IA) routes and one external (E2) route. In complex OSPF networks, a large number of external and interarea routes can needlessly weigh down some routers. Because Capetown is in a stub area, an area with one egress point, it does not need external routing information, or even interarea summaries. Capetown just needs a default route to the ABR, SanJose3.

By configuring Area 2 as a stub area, SanJose3 automatically propagates a default route into Area 2. Use the following commands to configure the stub area:

```
SanJose3(config)#router ospf 1
SanJose3(config-router)#area 2 stub
```

You must also configure Capetown:

```
Capetown(config)#router ospf 1
Capetown(config-router)#area 2 stub
```

Verify that Area 2 is a stub by issuing the **show ip ospf** command:

```
CapeTown#show ip ospf
 Routing Process "ospf 1" with ID 192.168.220.1
 Supports only single TOS(TOS0) routes
 SPF schedule delay 5 secs, Hold time between two SPFs 10 secs
 Minimum LSA interval 5 secs. Minimum LSA arrival 1 secs
```

```
Number of external LSA 0. Checksum Sum 0x0
Number of DCbitless external LSA 0
Number of DoNotAge external LSA 0
Number of areas in this router is 1. 0 normal 1 stub 0 nssa
External flood list length 0
    Area 2
        Number of interfaces in this area is 2
            It is a stub area
        Area has no authentication
        SPF algorithm executed 6 times
        Area ranges are
        Number of LSA 9. Checksum Sum 0x428E6
        Number of DCbitless LSA 0
        Number of indication LSA 0
        Number of DoNotAge LSA 0
        Flood list length 0
```

1. According to the output of this command, what type of OSPF area is Area 2?

_____

Now check Capetown's routing table. Note that a default route (0.0.0.0/0) has been generated by the stub's ABR (SanJose3) and now appears in Capetown's table.

```
CapeTown#show ip route

Gateway of last resort is 192.168.208.1 to network 0.0.0.0

     192.168.208.0/30 is subnetted, 1 subnets
C        192.168.208.0 is directly connected, Serial0/0
     192.168.64.0/32 is subnetted, 1 subnets
O IA     192.168.64.1 [110/66] via 192.168.208.1, 00:01:01,
         Serial0/0
C    192.168.216.0/24 is directly connected, FastEthernet0/0
     192.168.80.0/32 is subnetted, 1 subnets
O IA     192.168.80.1 [110/66] via 192.168.208.1, 00:01:01,
         Serial0/0
     192.168.96.0/32 is subnetted, 1 subnets
O IA     192.168.96.1 [110/66] via 192.168.208.1, 00:01:01,
         Serial0/0
     192.168.112.0/32 is subnetted, 1 subnets
O IA     192.168.112.1 [110/66] via 192.168.208.1, 00:01:02,
         Serial0/0
C    192.168.220.0/24 is directly connected, Loopback0
O IA 192.168.1.0/24 [110/65] via 192.168.208.1, 00:01:02,
         Serial0/0
     192.168.3.0/32 is subnetted, 1 subnets
O IA     192.168.3.1 [110/65] via 192.168.208.1, 00:01:03,
         Serial0/0
O*IA 0.0.0.0/0 [110/65] via 192.168.208.1, 00:01:03, Serial0/0
```

2. What type of OSPF route is Capetown's default route?

_____

Recall that interarea (IA) routes point to networks in different areas within the same OSPF autonomous system.

Because Area 2 is a stub area, all external routes (Type 5 LSAs) have been prevented from reaching internal routers.

3. Look carefully at Capetown's routing table. Does it still have a route to 10.0.0.0/8?

All external routes are filtered from stub areas and are replaced with a default route.

Step 4

You decide that stub area configuration is not making a significant-enough impact on Area 2. Because Capetown can use the default route to its ABR for all nonlocal area traffic, you decide to filter Type 3 and Type 4 interarea routes from Area 2. To do this, you must configure Area 2 as a totally stubby area, which is a Cisco proprietary feature.

Use the following commands on SanJose3, the ABR, to configure Area 2 as a totally stubby area:

```
SanJose3(config)#router ospf 1
SanJose3(config-router)#no area 2 stub
SanJose3(config-router)#area 2 stub no-summary
```

The **no-summary** keyword at the ABR keeps interarea routes from entering stub Area 2, creating a totally stubby area. Only the ABR needs the additional configuration. The role of Area 2 internal routers has not changed.

Return to Capetown and check its routing table:

```
CapeTown#show ip route

Gateway of last resort is 192.168.208.1 to network 0.0.0.0

     192.168.208.0/30 is subnetted, 1 subnets
C       192.168.208.0 is directly connected, Serial0/0
C    192.168.216.0/24 is directly connected, FastEthernet0/0
C    192.168.220.0/24 is directly connected, Loopback0
O*IA 0.0.0.0/0 [110/65] via 192.168.208.1, 00:00:25, Serial0/0
```

4. What has changed?

---

5. Does Area 2 still have connectivity to 10.0.0.0/8? Test with **ping 10.0.0.6**.

Interarea routes have also been replaced by a default route.

Capetown should get a positive response by forwarding ICMP requests to SanJose3 using the default route 0.0.0.0/0. SanJose3 has a default route to network 10.0.0.0/8, and SanJose1 has a directly connected route to 10.0.0.4/30 with the loopback interface 10.0.0.6/30.

Lab 5-3: Configuring an NSSA

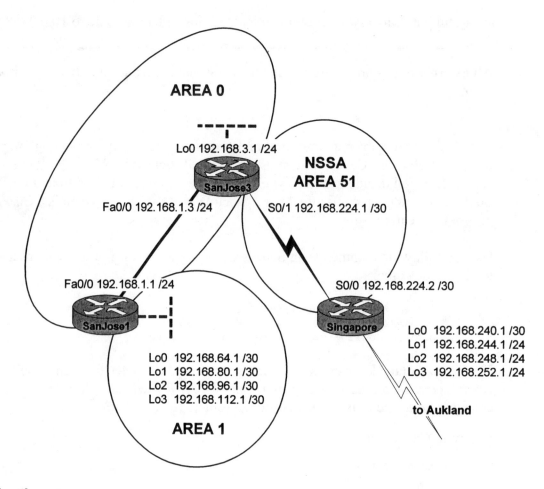

Objective

In this lab, you configure an OSPF NSSA in order to import external routing information while retaining the benefits of a stub area.

Scenario

The implementation of a totally stubby area in Area 2 was so successful that you want to implement it in Area 51 for efficient routing and greater route stability. A stub or totally stubby area won't work, because the Singapore router in Area 51 has the added responsibility of redistributing external routes from Auckland using Type 5 LSAs. To meet all your needs, you decide to configure Area 51 as an NSSA (Not So Stubby Area).

Step 1

Build and configure the network according to the diagram. Also configure multiarea OSPF according to the diagram (do not configure NSSA yet).
Note: This lab requires the use of subnet 0.

Configure each router with the loopback address indicated in the diagram. Be sure to configure SanJose1 and Singapore with additional loopbacks (Lo0, Lo1, Lo2, Lo3). On SanJose1, these loopback interfaces simulate the serial links to local San Jose sites: Westasman, Baypointe, Vista, and Eastasman. On Singapore, the loopbacks simulate Auckland networks.

Use **ping** and **show ip route** to test connectivity between all interfaces. Each router should be able to ping all network interfaces:

```
SanJose3#show ip route

     192.168.224.0/30 is subnetted, 1 subnets
C       192.168.224.0 is directly connected, Serial0/0
     192.168.64.0/32 is subnetted, 1 subnets
O IA    192.168.64.1 [110/2] via 192.168.1.1, 00:03:49,
        FastEthernet0/0
     192.168.80.0/32 is subnetted, 1 subnets
O IA    192.168.80.1 [110/2] via 192.168.1.1, 00:03:49,
        FastEthernet0/0
     192.168.96.0/32 is subnetted, 1 subnets
O IA    192.168.96.1 [110/2] via 192.168.1.1, 00:03:49,
        FastEthernet0/0
     192.168.112.0/32 is subnetted, 1 subnets
O IA    192.168.112.1 [110/2] via 192.168.1.1, 00:03:49,
        FastEthernet0/0
C    192.168.1.0/24 is directly connected, FastEthernet0/0
C    192.168.3.0/24 is directly connected, Loopback0
```

Step 2

Configure Singapore to redistribute connected routes into the OSPF domain:

```
Singapore(config)#router ospf 1
Singapore(config-router)#redistribute connected subnets
```

Check the routing tables of all three routers; they should be complete. SanJose1 and SanJose3 should also have Type 2 external routes to the Auckland networks.

```
SanJose1#show ip route

     192.168.224.0/30 is subnetted, 1 subnets
O IA    192.168.224.0 [110/782] via 192.168.1.3, 00:11:16,
        FastEthernet0/0
     192.168.240.0/30 is subnetted, 1 subnets
O E2    192.168.240.0 [110/20] via 192.168.1.3, 00:04:54,
        FastEthernet0/0
O E2 192.168.244.0/24 [110/20] via 192.168.1.3, 00:09:34,
        FastEthernet0/0
     192.168.64.0/30 is subnetted, 1 subnets
C       192.168.64.0 is directly connected, Loopback0
     192.168.80.0/30 is subnetted, 1 subnets
C       192.168.80.0 is directly connected, Loopback1
     192.168.96.0/30 is subnetted, 1 subnets
C       192.168.96.0 is directly connected, Loopback2
O E2 192.168.248.0/24 [110/20] via 192.168.1.3, 00:09:35,
        FastEthernet0/0
     192.168.112.0/30 is subnetted, 1 subnets
C       192.168.112.0 is directly connected, Loopback3
```

```
C     192.168.1.0/24 is directly connected, FastEthernet0/0
O E2 192.168.252.0/24 [110/20] via 192.168.1.3, 00:09:38,
      FastEthernet0/0
      192.168.3.0/32 is subnetted, 1 subnets
O        192.168.3.1 [110/2] via 192.168.1.3, 00:11:19,
      FastEthernet0/0
```

Step 3

Singapore has several interarea (IA) routes.

```
Singapore#show ip route

Gateway of last resort is not set

      192.168.224.0/30 is subnetted, 1 subnets
C        192.168.224.0 is directly connected, Serial0/0
      192.168.240.0/30 is subnetted, 1 subnets
C        192.168.240.0 is directly connected, Loopback0
C     192.168.244.0/24 is directly connected, Loopback1
      192.168.64.0/32 is subnetted, 1 subnets
O IA     192.168.64.1 [110/66] via 192.168.224.1, 00:00:48,
      Serial0/0
      192.168.80.0/32 is subnetted, 1 subnets
O IA     192.168.80.1 [110/66] via 192.168.224.1, 00:00:48,
      Serial0/0
      192.168.96.0/32 is subnetted, 1 subnets
O IA     192.168.96.1 [110/66] via 192.168.224.1, 00:00:49,
      Serial0/0
C     192.168.248.0/24 is directly connected, Loopback2
      192.168.112.0/32 is subnetted, 1 subnets
O IA     192.168.112.1 [110/66] via 192.168.224.1, 00:00:49,
      Serial0/0
O IA 192.168.1.0/24 [110/65] via 192.168.224.1, 00:00:49,
      Serial0/0
C     192.168.252.0/24 is directly connected, Loopback3
      192.168.3.0/32 is subnetted, 1 subnets
O IA     192.168.3.1 [110/65] via 192.168.224.1, 00:00:49,
      Serial0/0
```

In Lab 5-2, you minimized Capetown's table by configuring Area 2 as a stub. Attempt to repeat this configuration with the following commands on Singapore:

```
Singapore(config)#router ospf 1
Singapore(config-router)#area 51 stub
```

1. What does the router output when you enter this command?

Because Singapore imports routes that are external to OSPF, it is considered an ASBR. ASBRs cannot be members of a stub area; stub areas do not permit Type 5 LSAs. Issue the **show ip ospf database** command on Singapore.

```
Singapore#show ip ospf database

      OSPF Router with ID (192.168.252.1) (Process ID 1)

          Router Link States (Area 51)
```

```
Link ID          ADV Router       Age         Seq#        Checksum
      Link count
192.168.3.1      192.168.3.1      817         0x80000004 0xF239    2
192.168.252.1    192.168.252.1    1307        0x80000002 0xB918    2

                 Summary Net Link States (Area 51)

Link ID          ADV Router       Age         Seq#        Checksum
192.168.1.0      192.168.3.1      1262        0x80000003 0xABB6
192.168.3.1      192.168.3.1      1308        0x80000001 0x8FD1
192.168.64.1     192.168.3.1      1258        0x80000001 0xF72B
192.168.80.1     192.168.3.1      1258        0x80000001 0x47CB
192.168.96.1     192.168.3.1      1258        0x80000001 0x966C
192.168.112.1    192.168.3.1      1258        0x80000001 0xE50D

                 Type-5 AS External Link States

Link ID          ADV Router       Age         Seq#        Checksum Tag
192.168.224.0    192.168.252.1    429         0x80000001 0x7D74    0
192.168.240.0    192.168.252.1    432         0x80000001 0xCC15    0
192.168.244.0    192.168.252.1    713         0x80000001 0xB228    0
192.168.248.0    192.168.252.1    713         0x80000001 0x8650    0
192.168.252.0    192.168.252.1    713         0x80000001 0x5A78    0
```

2. According to the output of this command, what link IDs are included under Type 5 AS External Link States?

_____

All Auckland network routes (loopbacks) are Type5 external links.

The workaround for this situation is to configure Area 51 as an NSSA. Enter the following commands:

```
Singapore(config)#router ospf 1
Singapore(config-router)#area 51 nssa

SanJose3(config)#router ospf 1
SanJose3(config-router)#area 51 nssa
```

Now use the **show ip ospf database** command on Singapore. Because stub areas do not support Type 5 LSAs, external routes are redistributed and are advertised as Type 7 LSAs. The output of this command should verify that Type 5 LSAs have been replaced by Type 7 LSAs.

```
Singapore#show ip ospf database

        OSPF Router with ID (192.168.252.1) (Process ID 1)

                 Router Link States (Area 51)

Link ID          ADV Router       Age         Seq#        Checksum
      Link count
192.168.3.1      192.168.3.1      10          0x80000006 0x9A87    2
192.168.252.1    192.168.252.1    10          0x80000004 0x5B6E    2

                 Summary Net Link States (Area 51)
```

```
Link ID          ADV Router        Age       Seq#        Checksum
192.168.1.0      192.168.3.1       137       0x80000004  0x4F0C
192.168.3.1      192.168.3.1       137       0x80000002  0x3327
192.168.64.1     192.168.3.1       138       0x80000002  0x9B80
192.168.80.1     192.168.3.1       138       0x80000002  0xEA21
192.168.96.1     192.168.3.1       138       0x80000002  0x3AC1
192.168.112.1    192.168.3.1       138       0x80000002  0x8962
```

```
              Type-7 AS External Link States (Area 51)

Link ID          ADV Router        Age       Seq#        Checksum  Tag
192.168.224.0    192.168.252.1     19        0x80000001  0xA0FA    0
192.168.240.0    192.168.252.1     20        0x80000001  0xEF9B    0
192.168.244.0    192.168.252.1     21        0x80000001  0xD5AE    0
192.168.248.0    192.168.252.1     21        0x80000001  0xA9D6    0
192.168.252.0    192.168.252.1     21        0x80000001  0x7DFE    0
```

NSSA routers receive updates from the ABR the same way stub area routers do. Singapore's routing table should look similar to Capetown's when it was in a stub area (see Lab 5-2). SanJose3 continues to flood Area 51 with summary link LSAs (Type 3 and Type 4). Because your goal is to reduce the burden on Area 51 routers, you should reconfigure SanJose3 to filter interarea summary LSAs:

```
SanJose3(config)#router ospf 1
SanJose3(config-router)#area 51 nssa no-summary
```

Again, check Singapore's table:

```
Singapore#show ip route

Gateway of last resort is 192.168.224.1 to network 0.0.0.0

     192.168.224.0/30 is subnetted, 1 subnets
C       192.168.224.0 is directly connected, Serial0/0
     192.168.240.0/30 is subnetted, 1 subnets
C       192.168.240.0 is directly connected, Loopback0
C    192.168.244.0/24 is directly connected, Loopback1
C    192.168.248.0/24 is directly connected, Loopback2
C    192.168.252.0/24 is directly connected, Loopback3
O*IA 0.0.0.0/0 [110/65] via 192.168.224.1, 00:00:04, Serial0/0
```

3. What has changed?

All interarea (IA) routes are replaced with the 0.0.0.0/0 default route. Area 51 is now acting like Area 2 when it was configured as totally stubby (see Lab 5-2). The primary difference is that an NSSA can redistribute external routes.

NSSAs allow you to minimize OSPF link state databases within an area, yet still import external routes as Type 7 LSAs. The NSSA ABR (in this case, SanJose3) must convert these Type 7s into Type 5s, which will be flooded into Area 0. On SanJose3, issue the **show ip ospf database** command:

```
Singapore#show ip ospf database

        OSPF Router with ID (192.168.3.1) (Process ID 1)

                Router Link States (Area 0)

Link ID         ADV Router      Age         Seq#        Checksum Link
        count
192.168.3.1     192.168.3.1     170         0x80000007 0x45B2    2
192.168.112.1   192.168.112.1   1711        0x80000008 0x148A    1

                Net Link States (Area 0)

Link ID         ADV Router      Age         Seq#        Checksum
192.168.1.1     192.168.112.1   1712        0x80000001 0xA10A

                Summary Net Link States (Area 0)

Link ID         ADV Router      Age         Seq#        Checksum
192.168.64.1    192.168.112.1   1238        0x80000005 0xE7CA
192.168.80.1    192.168.112.1   1238        0x80000005 0x376B
192.168.96.1    192.168.112.1   1238        0x80000005 0x860C
192.168.112.1   192.168.112.1   1238        0x80000005 0xD5AC
192.168.224.0   192.168.3.1     1748        0x80000001 0x92E5

                Router Link States (Area 51)

Link ID         ADV Router      Age         Seq#        Checksum
        Link count
192.168.3.1     192.168.3.1     165         0x8000000B 0x908C    2
192.168.252.1   192.168.252.1   278         0x80000004 0x5B6E    2

                Summary Net Link States (Area 51)

Link ID         ADV Router      Age         Seq#        Checksum
0.0.0.0         192.168.3.1     172         0x80000001 0x12B6
```

```
           Type-7 AS External Link States (Area 51)

Link ID         ADV Router      Age         Seq#        Checksum Tag
192.168.224.0   192.168.252.1   287         0x80000001 0xA0FA    0
192.168.240.0   192.168.252.1   287         0x80000001 0xEF9B    0
192.168.244.0   192.168.252.1   287         0x80000001 0xD5AE    0
192.168.248.0   192.168.252.1   287         0x80000001 0xA9D6    0
192.168.252.0   192.168.252.1   287         0x80000001 0x7DFE    0

               Type-5 AS External Link States

Link ID         ADV Router      Age         Seq#        Checksum Tag
192.168.240.0   192.168.3.1     161         0x80000001 0x5A35    0
192.168.244.0   192.168.3.1     163         0x80000001 0x4048    0
192.168.248.0   192.168.3.1     163         0x80000001 0x1470    0
192.168.252.0   192.168.3.1     163         0x80000001 0xE798    0
```

4. Does SanJose3's database include link IDs that use Type 7 LSAs?

_____

5. Does SanJose3's database include link IDs that use Type 5 LSAs?

_____

Singapore3 converts the Type7 LSAs from Singapore and propagates them as Type 5 LSAs to SanJose1.

Issue the **show ip route** command on SanJose3:

```
SanJose3#show ip route

Gateway of last resort is not set

     192.168.224.0/30 is subnetted, 1 subnets
C       192.168.224.0 is directly connected, Serial0/0
     192.168.240.0/30 is subnetted, 1 subnets
O N2    192.168.240.0 [110/20] via 192.168.224.2, 00:03:23,
        Serial0/0
O N2 192.168.244.0/24 [110/20] via 192.168.224.2, 00:03:23,
        Serial0/0
     192.168.64.0/32 is subnetted, 1 subnets
O IA    192.168.64.1 [110/2] via 192.168.1.1, 00:03:23,
        FastEthernet0/0
     192.168.80.0/32 is subnetted, 1 subnets
O IA    192.168.80.1 [110/2] via 192.168.1.1, 00:03:23,
        FastEthernet0/0
     192.168.96.0/32 is subnetted, 1 subnets
O IA    192.168.96.1 [110/2] via 192.168.1.1, 00:03:24,
        FastEthernet0/0
O N2 192.168.248.0/24 [110/20] via 192.168.224.2, 00:03:24,
        Serial0/0
     192.168.112.0/32 is subnetted, 1 subnets
IA      192.168.112.1 [110/2] via 192.168.1.1, 00:03:30,
        FastEthernet0/0
C    192.168.1.0/24 is directly connected, FastEthernet0/0
O N2 192.168.252.0/24 [110/20] via 192.168.224.2, 00:03:30,
        Serial0/0
C    192.168.3.0/24 is directly connected, Loopback0
```

6. According to the output of this command, what kind of OSPF route is the external route to 192.168.248.0/24?

NSSA Type 2 (N2) routes are learned through Type 7 LSAs.

Finally, check SanJose1's routing table. The external route to 192.168.248.0/24 should still be installed. Issue the **show ip ospf database** command on SanJose1:

```
SanJose1#show ip ospf database

        OSPF Router with ID (192.168.112.1) (Process ID 1)

            Router Link States (Area 0)

Link ID         ADV Router      Age         Seq#        Checksum
    Link count
192.168.3.1     192.168.3.1     390         0x80000007 0x45B2    2
192.168.112.1   192.168.112.1   1931        0x80000008 0x148A    1

            Net Link States (Area 0)

Link ID         ADV Router      Age         Seq#        Checksum
```

```
        192.168.1.1      192.168.112.1   1931         0x80000001 0xA10A

                         Summary Net Link States (Area 0)

        Link ID          ADV Router      Age         Seq#       Checksum
        192.168.64.1     192.168.112.1   1456         0x80000005 0xE7CA
        192.168.80.1     192.168.112.1   1457         0x80000005 0x376B
        192.168.96.1     192.168.112.1   1457         0x80000005 0x860C
        192.168.112.1    192.168.112.1   1457         0x80000005 0xD5AC
        192.168.224.0    192.168.3.1     1967         0x80000001 0x92E5

                         Router Link States (Area 1)

        Link ID          ADV Router      Age         Seq#       Checksum
             Link count
        192.168.112.1    192.168.112.1   1457         0x80000006 0x39FE    4

                         Summary Net Link States (Area 1)

        Link ID          ADV Router      Age         Seq#       Checksum
        192.168.1.0      192.168.112.1   1924         0x80000009 0xA14D
        192.168.3.1      192.168.112.1   1919         0x80000001 0x9B57
        192.168.224.0    192.168.112.1   1919         0x80000001 0x9E6B

                         Summary ASB Link States (Area 1)

        Link ID          ADV Router      Age         Seq#       Checksum
        192.168.3.1      192.168.112.1   387          0x80000003 0x7F71
```

Type-5 AS External Link States

```
        Link ID          ADV Router      Age         Seq#       Checksum Tag
        192.168.240.0    192.168.3.1     383          0x80000001 0x5A35   0
        192.168.244.0    192.168.3.1     383          0x80000001 0x4048   0
        192.168.248.0    192.168.3.1     383          0x80000001 0x1470   0
192.168.252.0    192.168.3.1     384          0x80000001 0xE798   0
```

7. Does SanJose1's database include link IDs that use Type 7 LSAs?

---

8. Does SanJose1's database include link IDs that use Type 5 LSAs?

Because SanJose3 converts Type 7 LSAs to Type 5, SanJose1 is unaware of the NSSA configuration of Area 51.

```
SanJose1#show ip route

Gateway of last resort is not set

     192.168.224.0/30 is subnetted, 1 subnets
O IA    192.168.224.0 [110/782] via 192.168.1.3, 00:06:38,
        FastEthernet0/0
     192.168.240.0/30 is subnetted, 1 subnets
O E2    192.168.240.0 [110/20] via 192.168.1.3, 00:06:32,
        FastEthernet0/0
O E2 192.168.244.0/24 [110/20] via 192.168.1.3, 00:06:32,
        FastEthernet0/0
     192.168.64.0/30 is subnetted, 1 subnets
C       192.168.64.0 is directly connected, Loopback0
```

```
       192.168.80.0/30 is subnetted, 1 subnets
C         192.168.80.0 is directly connected, Loopback1
       192.168.96.0/30 is subnetted, 1 subnets
C         192.168.96.0 is directly connected, Loopback2
O E2 192.168.248.0/24 [110/20] via 192.168.1.3, 00:06:33,
       FastEthernet0/0
       192.168.112.0/30 is subnetted, 1 subnets
C         192.168.112.0 is directly connected, Loopback3
C      192.168.1.0/24 is directly connected, FastEthernet0/0
O E2 192.168.252.0/24 [110/20] via 192.168.1.3, 00:06:35,
       FastEthernet0/0
       192.168.3.0/32 is subnetted, 1 subnets
O         192.168.3.1 [110/2] via 192.168.1.3, 00:06:41,
       FastEthernet0/0
```

Lab 5-4: Configuring Virtual Links

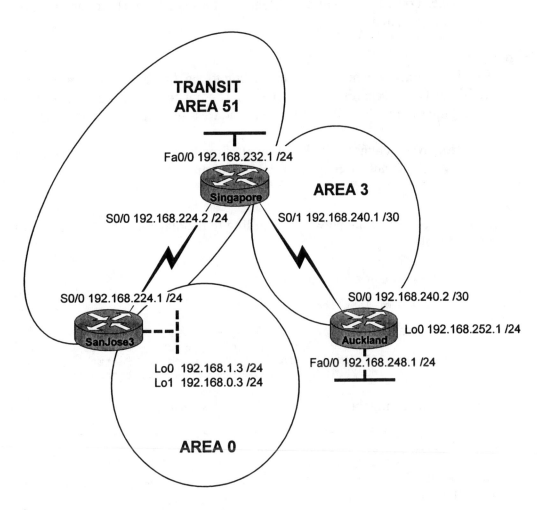

TRANSIT AREA 51

Fa0/0 192.168.232.1 /24

Singapore

AREA 3

S0/0 192.168.224.2 /24

S0/1 192.168.240.1 /30

S0/0 192.168.224.1 /24

S0/0 192.168.240.2 /30

SanJose3

Lo0 192.168.252.1 /24

Auckland

Fa0/0 192.168.248.1 /24

Lo0 192.168.1.3 /24
Lo1 192.168.0.3 /24

AREA 0

Objective

In this lab, you configure an OSPF virtual link so that a disconnected area can reach the backbone, as required by OSPF.

Scenario

At midnight, your pager goes off as you are sleeping in your San Jose home. You are informed that connectivity to Auckland and Singapore has been intermittent for several hours. You log on to the corporate network from home, run some diagnostics, and determine that you can't get to Auckland. Also, you notice that the Shortest Path First algorithm is being recalculated often on your core routers. The instability seems to be associated with the Asian region of your network. Singapore local time is approximately 4:30 p.m. You call the technical support lead in Singapore to ask if they are experiencing any network connectivity issues. He is disappointed that you noticed already, but he proudly says that he has added OSPF Area 3 in Auckland so that external routes do not need be redistributed. You agree that it would be best to include Auckland in the OSPF autonomous system, but you disagree that another area should be created. A teleconference is set for tomorrow, and you go about restoring connectivity and stability. A proper OSPF design has all areas adjacent to Area 0, but Area 3 is disconnected from the backbone. You will configure a virtual link through Area 51, connecting Area 3 to the backbone, Area 0.

Step 1

Build and configure the network according to the diagram. Also configure multiarea OSPF according to the diagram (do not configure the virtual link yet). Configure each router with the loopback address indicated in the diagram.

Use **ping** to test connectivity between all directly connected interfaces. Each router should be able to ping its serial link partner.

Step 2

After you configure the network according to the diagram, check Auckland's routing table:

```
Auckland#show ip route

Gateway of last resort is not set

     192.168.240.0/30 is subnetted, 1 subnets
C       192.168.240.0 is directly connected, Serial0/0
C    192.168.248.0/24 is directly connected, FastEthernet0/0
C    192.168.252.0/24 is directly connected, Loopback0
```

1. The routing table should be devoid of OSPF routes. Why?

_____

_____

Interarea traffic must transit the backbone area. Even though Area 51 and Area 3 are adjacent, they do not share OSPF routing updates.

Verify that Auckland has established a neighbor relationship with Singapore by using the **show ip ospf neighbor** command:

```
Auckland#show ip ospf neighbor

Neighbor ID     Pri   State       Dead Time  Address      Interface
192.168.240.1    1    FULL/       00:00:33   192.168.240.1 Serial0/0
```

2. What state exists between Singapore and Auckland?

_____

Singapore and Auckland should have successfully established adjacencies, shown as the "full" neighbor state.

Step 3

Because Area 3 is not connected to the backbone, OSPF routing is broken in this network. You must configure a virtual link, or drastically redesign the network, in order to make routing work. To quickly restore connectivity, you will configure a virtual link between Singapore (Area 3's ABR) and SanJose3 (Area 0's ABR). Thus, the transit area between Area 3 and Area 0 will be Area 51. Enter the following commands on Singapore:

```
Singapore(config)#router ospf 1
Singapore(config-router)#area 51 virtual-link 192.168.1.3
```

Note: You must specify SanJose3 by its router ID.

In order for the virtual link to function, you must configure both ends of the link. On SanJose3, issue the following commands:

```
SanJose3(config)#router ospf 1
SanJose3(config-router)#area 51 virtual-link 192.168.240.1
```

You can verify the creation of the virtual link by checking Auckland's routing table:

```
Auckland#show ip route

Gateway of last resort is not set

O IA 192.168.224.0/24 [110/845] via 192.168.240.1, 00:01:25,
        Serial0/0
     192.168.240.0/30 is subnetted, 1 subnets
C        192.168.240.0 is directly connected, Serial0/0
O IA 192.168.232.0/24 [110/65] via 192.168.240.1, 00:01:25,
        Serial0/0
C    192.168.248.0/24 is directly connected, FastEthernet0/0
     192.168.0.0/32 is subnetted, 1 subnets
O IA    192.168.0.3 [110/846] via 192.168.240.1, 00:00:35,
        Serial0/0
     192.168.1.0/32 is subnetted, 1 subnets
O IA    192.168.1.3 [110/846] via 192.168.240.1, 00:00:35,
        Serial0/0
C    192.168.252.0/24 is directly connected, Loopback0
```

If it receives OSPF routes, the virtual link is operational.
Alternatively, you can issue the command **show ip ospf virtual-links** on Singapore:

```
Singapore#show ip ospf virtual-links
Virtual Link OSPF_VL0 to router 192.168.1.3 is up
  Run as demand circuit
  DoNotAge LSA allowed.
  Transit area 51, via interface Serial0/0, Cost of using 781
  Transmit Delay is 1 sec, State POINT_TO_POINT,
  Timer intervals configured, Hello 10, Dead 40, Wait 40,
      Retransmit 5
    Hello due in 00:00:00
  Adjacency State FULL (Hello suppressed)
  Index 1/3, retransmission queue length 0, number of
  retransmission 1
  First 0x0(0)/0x0(0) Next 0x0(0)/0x0(0)
  Last retransmission scan length is 1, maximum is 1
  Last retransmission scan time is 0 msec, maximum is 0 msec
```

3. According to the output of this command, what is the state of the virtual link?

_____

OSPF Challenge Lab

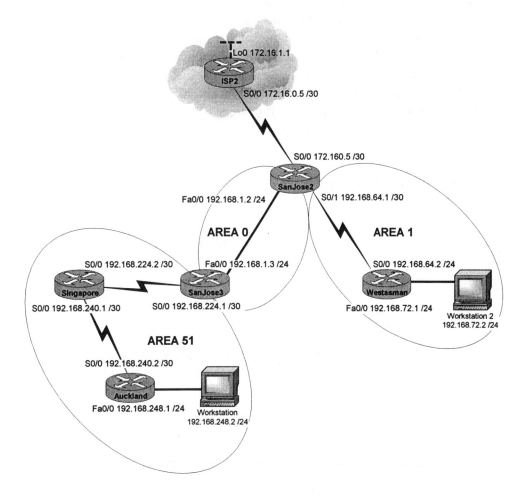

Objective

In this lab, you create a multiarea OSPF autonomous system that includes a totally stubby area and a persistent default route toward the ISP.

Scenario

As the Enterprise Network Administrator for International Travel Agency, you are responsible for designing and implementing internetwork connectivity. To ensure success by reducing complexity, you start scaling the network by connecting only the Asia region and one local site, West Tasman, to the San Jose corporate headquarters and ISP2. When you are satisfied with the results, you will implement all other regions and sites.

Design Considerations

At this point, West Tasman is in stub Area 1 with one egress point and no need to redistribute external routes. The router at West Tasman has been in service for several years and might not be able to keep up with a large OSPF internetwork. Your autonomous system also has only one egress point to the Internet. Instead of the administrative burden of many static routes, you want a stable default route advertised through OSPF, but you are concerned about route flapping if your WAN link to ISP2 is unstable. When provisioning the network, you upgraded the memory and processor on SanJose2, intending it to be the ASBR and the DR for any area it is a member of.

Implementation Requirements

- Configure Area 1 as a Totally Stubby Area.
- Advertise a persistent default route from SanJose2 through OSPF.
- SanJose2 will always be the DR in Area 0.
- SanJose3 will never be the DR in Area 0.

Implementation Completion Tests

- Successful pings to ISP2 from workstation1 and workstation2.
- Only a default route in the Westasman route table.
- The **show** command verifies that SanJose2 is DR.
- Two minutes after a WAN link failure (disconnect the serial cable from ISP2), an E2 default route is still present in Auckland.

Lab 6-1: Configuring EIGRP with IGRP

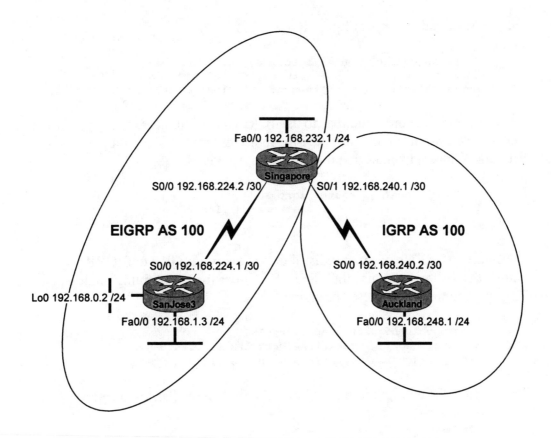

Objective

In this lab, you configure both EIGRP and IGRP within the International Travel Agency WAN and observe the automatic sharing of route information between both protocols.

Scenario

The International Travel Agency migrated from IGRP to EIGRP between its overseas headquarters and its North American headquarters. However, the Auckland headquarters is still unable to support EIGRP and must continue running IGRP for the time being. You must configure EIGRP on the SanJose3 and Singapore routers so that they can exchange information with the Auckland router.

Step 1

Build and configure the network according to the diagram, but do not configure EIGRP or IGRP yet.

Use **ping** to verify your work and test connectivity between serial interfaces. SanJose3 should be unable to ping Auckland until a routing protocol is enabled.

Step 2

On the Auckland router, configure IGRP for AS 100:

```
Auckland(config)#router igrp 100
Auckland(config-router)#network 192.168.248.0
Auckland(config-router)#network 192.168.240.0
```

Because the Singapore router has to use IGRP to communicate with the Auckland router, you must also configure the Singapore router for IGRP, but only on the network connected via the serial interface to Auckland.

```
Singapore(config)#router igrp 100
Singapore(config-router)#network 192.168.240.0
```

Step 3

Configure EIGRP. In order to redistribute routes from IGRP to EIGRP automatically, you must use the same AS number for each routing process. On the Singapore router, enter these commands:

```
Singapore(config)#router eigrp 100
Singapore(config-router)#network 192.168.224.0
Singapore(config-router)#network 192.168.0.0
```

To complete the configuration, configure EIGRP on the SanJose3 router:

```
SanJose3(config)#router eigrp 100
SanJose3(config)#network 192.168.224.0
SanJose3(config-router)#network 192.168.0.0
SanJose3(config-router)#network 192.168.1.0
```

Step 4

After you enable routing processes on each of the three routers, verify their operation using the **show ip route** command on the Singapore router. The Singapore router should have routes to all networks.

1. Based on the output of this command, which of the routes was learned via EIGRP?

_____

2. Which route was learned via IGRP?

_____

Now issue the **show ip route** command on the SanJose3 router, the EIGRP router. The SanJose3 router received EIGRP routes that are internal to the EIGRP domain (192.168.224.0), as well as routes that are external to the domain (192.168.240.0 and 192.168.248.0). Notice that these routes are differentiated in the table; internally learned routes have a D, and externally learned routes are denoted by a D EX.

3. What is the administrative distance of an internal EIGRP route?

_____

4. What is the administrative distance of an external EIGRP route?

_____

   Now issue the **show ip route** command on the Auckland router, the IGRP router.

5. Can you tell which IGRP routes are internal and which are external based on the information in this table?

_____

6. What is the administrative distance of an IGRP route?

_____

Step 5

   Now that EIGRP and IGRP are configured, use **show** commands to view EIGRP's neighbor and topology tables on the SanJose3 router.

   From the SanJose3 router, issue the **show** command to view the neighbor table:

```
SanJose3#show ip eigrp neighbor
```

7. Why isn't the Auckland router an EIGRP neighbor of the SanJose3 router?

_____

   To view the topology table, issue the **show ip eigrp topology all-links** command.

8. How many routers are in passive mode?

_____

   To view more-specific information about a topology table entry, use an IP address with this command:

```
SanJose3#show ip eigrp topology 192.168.248.0
```

9. Based on the output of this command, can you tell what external protocol originated this route to 192.168.248.0?

_____

10. Can you tell which router originated the route?

_____

   Finally, you can use **show** commands to view key EIGRP statistics. On the SanJose3 router, issue the **show ip eigrp traffic** command.

11. How many Hellos has the SanJose3 router received? How many has it sent?

_____

Lab 6-2: Configuring EIGRP Fault Tolerance

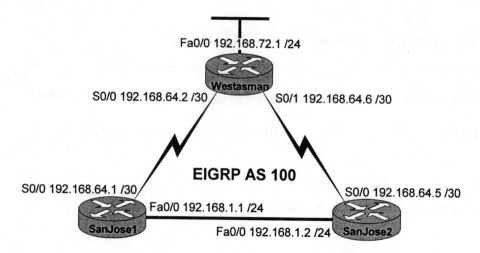

Objective

In this lab, you configure EIGRP over a full-mesh topology so that you can test and observe DUAL replace a successor with a feasible successor after a link failure.

Scenario

The International Travel Agency wants to run EIGRP on its core, branch, and regional routers. You are asked to configure EIGRP and test its ability to install alternate routes in the event of link failure.

Step 1

Build and configure the network according to the diagram, configuring EIGRP as indicated for AS 100.

Check each serial interface's bandwidth and change to 1544 if necessary. Use the **show interface** command to verify the configuration.

Use **ping** and **show ip route** to verify your work and test connectivity between all routers.

Step 2

Verify that EIGRP maintains all routes to destination networks in its topology table.

From the SanJose2 router, issue the **show ip eigrp topology all-links** command:

```
SanJose2#show ip eigrp topology all-links
IP-EIGRP Topology Table for AS(100)/ID(192.168.64.5)

Codes: P - Passive, A - Active, U - Update, Q - Query, R - Reply,
       r - Reply status

P 192.168.72.0/24, 1 successors, FD is 20514560, serno 10
        via 192.168.64.6 (20514560/28160), Serial0/0
        via 192.168.1.1 (20517120/20514560), FastEthernet0/0
P 192.168.64.0/30, 1 successors, FD is 21024000, serno 11
        via 192.168.64.6 (21024000/2169856), Serial0/0
P 192.168.64.0/24, 1 successors, FD is 20512000, serno 4
        via Summary (20512000/0), Null0
        via 192.168.1.1 (20514560/20512000), FastEthernet0/0
P 192.168.64.4/30, 1 successors, FD is 20512000, serno 3
        via Connected, Serial0/0
P 192.168.1.0/24, 0 successors, FD is Inaccessible, serno 0
        via 192.168.64.6 (21026560/2172416), Serial0/0
```

The SanJose2 router's topology table includes two paths to the 192.168.72.0 network. Use the **show ip route** command to determine which of the two is installed in SanJose2's routing table.

1. Which route is installed?

---

2. According to the output of the **show ip eigrp topology all-links** command, what is the feasible distance (FD) for the route 192.168.72.0?

Both paths to 192.168.72.0 are listed in the topology table with their computed distance and reported distance in parentheses. Computed distance is listed first.

3. What is the reported distance (RD) of the route to 192.168.72.0 via 192.168.1.1?

---

4. Is this RD greater than, less than, or equal to the route's FD?

Step 3

You must use the **debug eigrp fsm** command to observe how EIGRP deals with the loss of a successor to a route.

On the SanJose2 router, issue the command **debug eigrp fsm**.

Next, shut down or unplug the SanJose2 router's serial connection. This causes the SanJose2 router to lose its preferred route to 192.168.72.0 via 192.168.64.6.

Examine the **debug eigrp fsm** output for information regarding the route to 192.168.72.0, as shown in this example:

```
0:25:25: %LINK-3-UPDOWN: Interface Serial0/0, changed state to
    down
00:25:25: DUAL: Find FS for dest 192.168.72.0/24. FD is 20514560,
    RD is 20514560
00:25:25: DUAL:        192.168.64.6 metric 4294967295/4294967295
00:25:25: DUAL:        192.168.1.1 metric 20517120/20514560 not
    found Dmin is 20517120
00:25:25: DUAL: Dest 192.168.72.0/24 entering active state.
00:25:25: DUAL: Set reply-status table. Count is 1.
00:25:25: DUAL: Not doing split horizon
00:25:25: DUAL: dual_rcvreply(): 192.168.72.0/24 via 192.168.1.1
    metric 20517120/20514560
00:25:25: DUAL: Count is 1
00:25:25: DUAL: Clearing handle 0, count is now 0
00:25:25: DUAL: Freeing reply status table
00:25:25: DUAL: Find FS for dest 192.168.72.0/24. FD is
    4294967295, RD is 4294967295 found
00:25:25: DUAL: Removing dest 192.168.72.0/24, nexthop
    192.168.64.6
00:25:25: DUAL: RT installed 192.168.72.0/24 via 192.168.1.1
00:25:25: DUAL: Send update about 192.168.72.0/24.  Reason: metric
    chg
00:25:25: DUAL: Send update about 192.168.72.0/24.  Reason: new if
```

The highlighted portion of the sample output shows DUAL attempting to locate a feasible successor (FS) for 192.168.72.0. In this case, DUAL failed to find a feasible successor, and the router entered the active state. After querying its EIGRP neighbors, SanJose2 locates and installs a route to 192.168.72.0/24 via 192.168.1.1.

Step 4

Verify that the new route has been installed by using the **show ip route** command.

Bring the SanJose2 router serial interface back up. You will see 192.168.64.6 restored as the preferred route to the 192.168.72.0 network.

Lab 6-3: Configuring EIGRP Summarization

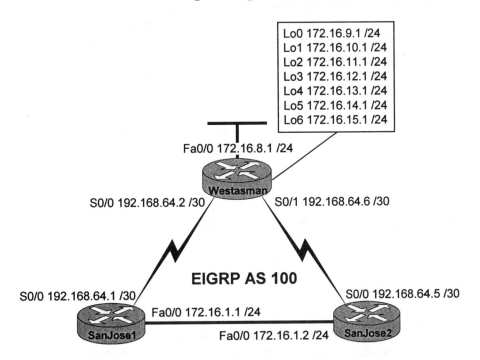

Objective

In this lab, you configure EIGRP to test its operation over discontiguous subnets by disabling automatic route summarization. Then you manually configure EIGRP to use specific summary routes.

Scenario

The International Travel Agency uses VLSM to conserve IP addresses. All LANs are addressed using contiguous subnets, but the company would like to examine the effects of discontiguous subnets using EIGRP for future reference. The existence of multiple networks is simulated by loopback interfaces on the Westasman router. The WAN links are addressed using 192.168.64.0 with a 30-bit mask.

Because this scheme creates discontiguous subnets, the default summarization behavior of EIGRP should result in incomplete routing tables. The problem should be resolved by disabling EIGRP's default summarization while maintaining a route summary at the Westasman router with manual route summarization.

Step 1

Build and configure the network according to the diagram. This configuration requires the use of subnet 0, so you might need to enter the **ip subnet- zero** command, depending on which IOS version you use. Configure the Westasman router with seven loopback interfaces using the IP addresses from the diagram. These interfaces simulate the existence of multiple networks behind the Westasman router. Configure EIGRP as indicated for AS 100.

Use **ping** to verify that all serial interfaces can ping each other. *Note:* Until you perform additional configurations, not all networks will appear in each router's routing table.

Step 2

Use **show ip route** to check SanJose1's routing table.

1. Which routes are missing?

_____

The SanJose 1 router has installed a "summary route" to network 172.16.0.0 /16 via Null0. EIGRP routers create these summary routes automatically. Because the local router, in this case, the SanJose1 router, has generated the summary, there is no next hop for the route. Thus, the SanJose1 router maps this summary route to its null interface.

2. Look again at SanJose1's routing table. What is the subnet mask for the route to 192.168.64.0?

_____

Check Westasman's routing table.

3. Which route is missing?

_____

Examine SanJose2's routing table.

4. Which routes are missing?

_____

In order to make these routing tables complete, EIGRP cannot automatically summarize routes based on classful boundaries.

Step 3

In this step, you disable EIGRP's automatic summarization feature.

On each router, issue these commands:

```
Westasman(config)#router eigrp 100
Westasman(config-router)#no auto-summary
```

After you issue these commands on all three routers, return to the SanJose1 router and type the **show ip route** command.

5. What has changed in SanJose1's routing table?

_____

All three routers should now have complete routing tables.

Step 4

Now that autosummarization is disabled, the International Travel Agency's routers should build complete routing tables. Unfortunately, this would mean that the Westasman router would be advertising eight routes that should be summarized for efficiency. Use EIGRP's manual summarization feature to summarize these addresses.

The Westasman router should be advertising the existence of eight subnets:

> 172.16.8.0
> 172.16.9.0
> 172.16.10.0
> 172.16.11.0
> 172.16.12.0
> 172.16.13.0
> 172.16.14.0
> 172.16.15.0

The first 21 bits of these addresses are the same, so a summary route for all subnets can be created using a /21 prefix (255.255.248.0 in dotted-decimal notation).

Because the Westasman router must advertise the summary route to the SanJose1 and SanJose2 routers, enter the following commands on the Westasman router:

```
Westasman(config)#interface s0/0
Westasman(config-if)#ip summary-address eigrp 100 172.16.8.0
     255.255.248.0
Westasman(config-if)#interface s0/1
Westasman(config-if)#ip summary-address eigrp 100 172.16.8.0
     255.255.248.0
```

These commands configure EIGRP to advertise summary routes for AS 100 via the serial 0 and 1 interfaces. Verify this configuration by issuing the **show ip protocols** command.

6. Which metric is the Westasman router using for its address summarization?

_____

    After you verify manual address summarization on the Westasman router, check
    the routing tables on the SanJose1 and SanJose2 routers.

7. What has happened in RTA's table since you looked at it in Step 3?

_____

    From the SanJose1 or SanJose2 router, verify that you can ping 172.16.8.1.

    You should be able to ping 172.16.15.1 from the SanJose1 router.

8. Is there a route to 172.16.15.0 in the SanJose1 router's routing table? Explain.

_____

EIGRP Challenge Lab

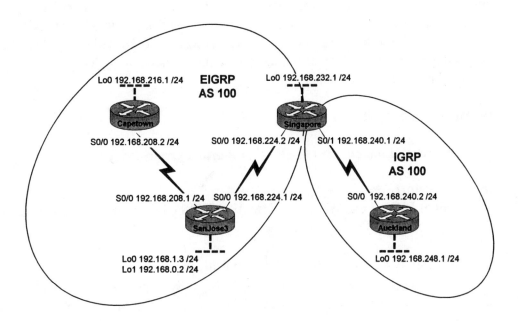

Objective

In this lab, you configure an International Travel Agency EIGRP WAN link with one IGRP segment within the same autonomous system. You also use EIGRP interface summarization to reduce the number of routes in an EIGRP routing table.

Scenario

The International Travel Agency is migrating from IGRP to EIGRP between its overseas headquarters and its North American headquarters. Unfortunately, the Auckland headquarters must continue running IGRP between it and Singapore. To help reduce the EIGRP routing table of the SanJose3 router, the Singapore router should be configured to advertise only a summary of the Auckland addresses. Then both the SanJose3 and Capetown routers would have summary Auckland addresses and smaller routing tables.

Design Considerations

Before you begin this lab, it is recommended that you reload each router after erasing its startup configuration. This prevents you from having problems caused by residual configurations. It is also recommended that you build and configure the network according to the diagram, but don't configure EIGRP or IGRP until you can verify and test connectivity between directly connected networks. The respective loopback addresses simulate local networks, so no physical connections need to be made.

Implementation Completion Tests

- A successful ping to every network (interface) from every router.

Capture Files/Printouts

After initial EIGRP and IGRP configuration, but before interface summarization, capture or print the following output:

- **show run** and **show ip route** for each router.
- **show ip eigrp neighbor** of the SanJose3 and Singapore routers.
- **show ip eigrp topology all-links** of the SanJose3 and Singapore routers.

After interface summarization, capture or print the following output:

- **show run** and **show ip route** of the Singapore router.
- **show ip route** of the SanJose3 and Capetown routers.

Lab 7-1: Configuring Distribute Lists and Passive Interfaces

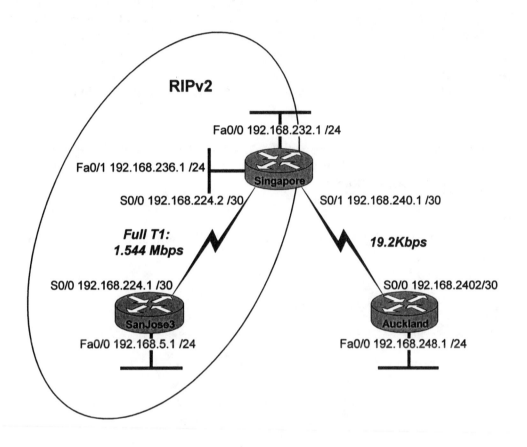

Objective

In this lab, you configure a combination of advanced routing features to optimize routing. These features include distribute lists, passive interfaces, default routes, and route redistribution.

Scenario

International Travel Agency (ITA) uses RIPv2 for dynamic routing. You do a performance analysis to determine whether RIPv2 is optimized.

A very slow 19.2 Kbps link is used to connect Singapore and Auckland until you can provision a faster link. To reduce traffic, you would like to avoid dynamic routing on this link.

You notice that one of the LANs with enterprise servers is near saturation. To reduce traffic, you decide to filter RIPv2 updates from entering SanJose3's 192.168.5.0/24 Ethernet LAN because the updates serve no purpose.

ITA has a large research and development division in Singapore. The R&D engineers are on LAN 192.168.236.0 /24. The R&D managers on the 192.168.232.0 /24 LAN need access to this experimental network, but you also want this LAN to be "invisible" to the rest of the company. Also, the two R&D LANs have many UNIX hosts that need to exchange RIPv2 updates with the Singapore router.

Step 1

Build and configure the network according to the diagram, but do not configure RIPv2 yet.

Use ping to verify your work and test connectivity between the serial interfaces. (*Note:* Auckland should not be able to ping SanJose3 until you have made additional configurations.)

Step 2

On SanJose3, configure RIPv2 to advertise both connected networks, as shown here:

```
SanJose3(config)#router rip
SanJose3(config-router)#version 2
SanJose3(config-router)#network 192.168.224.0
SanJose3(config-router)#network 192.168.5.0
```

No routers or hosts on SanJose3's Ethernet LAN need RIPv2 advertisements. However, if you don't include the 192.168.5.0 network in the RIPv2 configuration, SanJose3 will not advertise the network to Singapore. However, you can configure FastEthernet 0/0 as a passive interface, keeping FastEthernet 0/0 from sending RIPv2 updates. Use the following commands:

```
SanJose3(config)#router rip
SanJose3(config-router)#passive-interface fastethernet0/0
```

RIPv2 updates will no longer be sent via E0.

Step 3

Now configure RIPv2 on Singapore. At this point, enable RIPv2 only on the 192.168.224.0 /30 network so that Singapore can exchange routing information with SanJose3:

```
Singapore(config)#router rip
Singapore(config-router)#version 2
Singapore(config-router)#network 192.168.224.0
```

After you enter this RIPv2 configuration on Singapore, check SanJose3's routing table with the **show ip route** command. Note that SanJose3 has not learned any routes via RIPv2:

```
SanJose3#show ip route
<output omitted>
C    172.16.0.0/24 is directly connected, FastEthernet0/0
C    192.168.224.0/24 is directly connected, Serial0/0
```

1. Why hasn't SanJose3 learned about 192.168.232.0 /24 and 192.168.236.0 /24?

_____

_____

RIP has not been configured on SanJose3 to advertise the Ethernet networks. Also, RIP will not advertise a route for 192.168.224.0/30 out interface serial 0/0, where the network resides.

Step 4

After you review network requirements, you decide to enable RIPv2 on Singapore's FastEthernet 0/0 and FastEthernet 0/1 so that UNIX hosts on these LANs can receive routing information:

```
Singapore(config)#router rip
Singapore(config-router)#network 192.168.232.0
Singapore(config-router)#network 192.168.236.0
```

RIPv2 is now sending updates to these networks, as required by the UNIX hosts. Check SanJose3's table again:

```
SanJose3#show ip route

Gateway of last resort is not set

     192.168.224.0/30 is subnetted, 1 subnets
C       192.168.224.0 is directly connected, Serial0/0
C    192.168.5.0/24 is directly connected, FastEthernet0/0
R    192.168.232.0/24 [120/1] via 192.168.224.2, 00:00:13,
        Serial0/0
R    192.168.236.0/24 [120/1] via 192.168.224.2, 00:00:09,
        Serial0/0
```

The **network** command enables RIP updates on interfaces within that major network and advertises those networks out all other RIP-enabled interfaces. SanJose3 now has routes to 192.168.232.0 /24 (which is good) and 192.168.236.0 /24 (which is bad). Remember that you want to keep this network invisible to the rest of the company.

Step 5

To stop Singapore from sending updates about 192.168.236.0 /24 (without disabling RIPv2 for that network), you can remove it from outgoing updates with the **distribute-list** command. Distribute lists allow you to filter the contents of incoming or outgoing routing updates.

Because you want to filter 192.168.236.0 /24 from outgoing updates to all their routers, use the following commands:

```
Singapore(config)#access-list 1 deny 192.168.236.0
Singapore(config)#access-list 1 permit any
Singapore(config)#router rip
Singapore(config-router)#distribute-list 1 out
```

Verify that this filter has been applied by issuing the **show ip protocols** command on Singapore.

```
Singapore#show ip protocol
Routing Protocol is "rip"
  Sending updates every 30 seconds, next due in 4 seconds
  Invalid after 180 seconds, hold down 180, flushed after 240
  Outgoing update filter list for all interfaces is 1
  Incoming update filter list for all interfaces is
  Redistributing: rip
  Default version control: send version 2, receive version 2
    Interface        Send  Recv  Triggered RIP  Key-chain
    FastEthernet0/0   2     2
    Serial0/0         2     2
    FastEthernet0/1   2     2
  Routing for Networks:
    192.168.224.0
    192.168.232.0
    192.168.236.0
  Passive Interface(s):
    Serial0/1
  Routing Information Sources:
    Gateway          Distance       Last Update
    192.168.224.1       120         00:00:03
  Distance: (default is 120)
```

2. According to the output of this command, which interface is the outgoing update filter list applied to?

_____

You should see that the list is applied to all RIP-enabled interfaces.

With the distribute list configured on Singapore, return to SanJose3 and flush the routing table with the **clear ip route *** command. Wait at least 5 seconds, and then use **show ip route** to check SanJose3's table:

```
SanJose3#show ip route

Gateway of last resort is not set

     192.168.224.0/30 is subnetted, 1 subnets
C       192.168.224.0 is directly connected, Serial0/0
C    192.168.5.0/24 is directly connected, FastEthernet0/0
R    192.168.232.0/24 [120/1] via 192.168.224.2, 00:00:01,
     Serial0/0
```

3. Is the route to 192.168.236.0 /24 in SanJose3's table? Is the route to 192.168.232.0 /24 in SanJose3's table?

The distribute list should have removed 192.168.236.0/24 from further RIP updates. 192.168.232.0/24 should be the only RIP route in SanJose3's table at this point.

Step 6

SanJose3's table is almost complete, but it does not yet include a route to 192.168.240.0 /30, which is directly connected to Singapore. You could enter a **network** command in Singapore's RIPv2 configuration so that it will advertise this network. Of course, you do not want RIPv2 updates sent out the 19.2 Kbps link, so you would have to place Singapore's S0/0 into passive mode. But there is another alternative. You can configure Singapore to redistribute connected networks into RIPv2. Enter the following commands on Singapore:

```
Singapore(config)#router rip
Singapore(config-router)#redistribute connected
Singapore(config-router)#no auto-summary
```

When you issue these commands, Singapore imports all directly connected routes into the RIP process. Thus, 192.168.240.0 /30 will be redistributed into RIPv2 and sent to SanJose3 as part of each RIPv2 update. Verify your configuration by issuing the following command on Singapore:

```
Singapore #show ip route 192.168.240.1
Routing entry for 192.168.1.0/30
  Known via "connected", distance 0, metric 0 (connected,
      via interface)
  Redistributing via rip
  Advertised by rip
  Routing Descriptor Blocks:
  * directly connected, via Serial0/0
      Route metric is 0, traffic share count is 1
```

The output of this command should confirm that this connected route is being redistributed and advertised by RIPv2.

Check SanJose3's routing table:

```
SanJose3#show ip route

Gateway of last resort is not set

     192.168.224.0/30 is subnetted, 1 subnets
C       192.168.224.0 is directly connected, Serial0/0
     192.168.240.0/30 is subnetted, 1 subnets
R       192.168.240.0 [120/1] via 192.168.224.2, 00:00:02,
       Serial0/0
C     192.168.5.0/24 is directly connected, FastEthernet0/0
R     192.168.232.0/24 [120/1] via 192.168.224.2, 00:00:02,
       Serial0/0
```

SanJose3 should now have RIPv2 routes to both 192.168.240.0 /30 and 192.168.232.0 /24.

Step 7

With routing between Singapore and SanJose3 almost complete, you will turn your attention to Auckland. Because you are avoiding dynamic routing on Auckland's WAN link, you decide to use a static route.

Auckland is a stub network. It has only one exit point to the rest of the world. In this situation, you can configure a static default route that will work for all nonlocal traffic:

```
Auckland(config)#ip route 0.0.0.0 0.0.0.0 192.168.240.1
```

Verify that Auckland is using a default route. First, from SanJose3's console, enter the **debug ip packet** command. Leave SanJose3's console session open while you return to Auckland. From Auckland's console, ping SanJose3's FastEthernet 0/0 at 192.168.5.1.

```
SanJose3#debug ip packet
IP packet debugging is on
00:53:31: IP: s=192.168.240.2 (Serial0/0), d=192.168.5.1, len 100,
     rcvd 4
00:53:31: IP: s=192.168.5.1 (local), d=192.168.240.2 (Serial0/0),
     len 100, sending
```

These pings should be successful. *Note:* SanJose3's debug output reports that the pings have been received and replied to.

Next, ping SanJose3 using extended **ping** commands. (You invoke extended ping by typing ping and pressing Enter in privileged mode.) Using extended commands, source the ping from Auckland's FastEthernet 0/0 address, 192.168.248.1:

```
Auckland#ping
Protocol [ip]: ip
Target IP address: 192.168.5.1
Repeat count [5]: 5
Datagram size [100]: 100
Timeout in seconds [2]: 2
Extended commands [n]: y
Source address or interface: 192.168.248.1
Type of service [0]: 0
Set DF bit in IP header? [no]: no
Validate reply data? [no]: no
Data pattern [0xABCD]: 0xABCD
Loose, Strict, Record, Timestamp, Verbose[none]: none
Sweep range of sizes [n]: n
```

4. Were these pings successful?

Check the **debug ip packet** output on SanJose3:

```
SanJose3#debug ip packet
IP packet debugging is on
00:56:53: IP: s=192.168.248.1 (Serial0/0), d=192.168.5.1, len 100,
     rcvd 4
00:56:53: IP: s=192.168.5.1 (local), d=192.168.248.1, len 100,
     unroutable
```

5. You should see that the pings (ICMP echo requests) arrived. Why didn't SanJose3 respond?

_____

_____

6. Check SanJose3's routing table. Does SanJose3 have a route to the 192.168.248.0/24 network?

_____

At this point, SanJose3 does not have a route to network 192.168.248.0/24 or a default route for unknown destinations.

Step 8

In order for Singapore and SanJose3 to route to 192.168.248.0 /24, you must configure a static route. You have decided to configure the static route on Singapore and then let Singapore propagate this route to other routers (SanJose3) dynamically. (This will save you from the task of entering a static route on every router.) Enter the following command on Singapore:

```
Singapore(config)#ip route 192.168.248.0 255.255.255.0
        192.168.240.2
```

This command configures a static route for the 192.168.248.0 /24 network using Auckland's S0 as the next hop.

In order for Singapore to dynamically update SanJose3 with this information, you must configure RIPv2 to redistribute static routes on Singapore. Issue the following commands:

```
Singapore(config)#router rip
Singapore(config-router)#redistribute static
```

Finally, check SanJose3's table:

```
SanJose3#show ip route

Gateway of last resort is not set

     192.168.224.0/30 is subnetted, 1 subnets
C       192.168.224.0 is directly connected, Serial0/0
     192.168.240.0/30 is subnetted, 1 subnets
R       192.168.240.0 [120/1] via 192.168.224.2, 00:00:01,
```

```
        Serial0/0
C       192.168.5.0/24 is directly connected, FastEthernet0/0
R       192.168.232.0/24 [120/1] via 192.168.224.2, 00:00:02,
        Serial0/0
R       192.168.248.0/24 [120/1] via 192.168.224.2, 00:00:02,
        Serial0/0
```

It should now be complete. Verify connectivity with an extended ping from SanJose3 FastEthernet 0/0 to Auckland's FastEthernet 0/0.

Lab 7-2: Configuring Route Maps

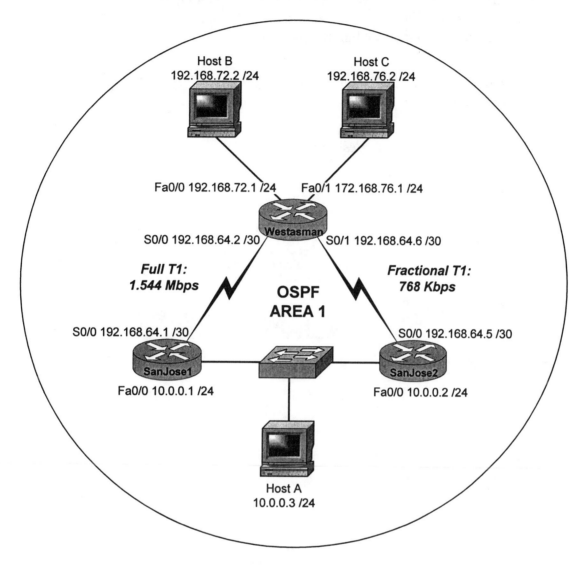

Objective

In this lab, you apply a routing policy by configuring a route map.

Scenario

International Travel Agency maintains two WAN links from the West Tasman site to its core network 10.0.0.0 /24. One link is full T1 (1.544 Mbps), and the other is a fractional T1 with a capacity of 768 Kbps. Under OSPF, West Tasman prefers the T1 link by virtue of its higher bandwidth (and lower cost). However, the Network Operations Center has decreed that all traffic from the 192.168.72.0 LAN bound to 10.0.0.0 /24 should use the slower fractional T1 link until further notice. You are to apply this policy by configuring a route map on the West Tasman router.

Step 1

Build and configure the network according to the diagram. Configure all interfaces for OSPF area 0. Configure Host A and Host B with IP addresses and default gateways as indicated in the diagram.

Use ping and **show ip route** to verify your work and test connectivity between all interfaces and hosts.

Step 2

Check the routing table on Westasman:

```
Westasman#show ip route

Gateway of last resort is not set

C    192.168.72.0/24 is directly connected, FastEthernet0/0
C    192.168.76.0/24 is directly connected, FastEthernet0/1
     192.168.64.0/30 is subnetted, 2 subnets
C       192.168.64.0 is directly connected, Serial0/0
C       192.168.64.4 is directly connected, Serial0/1
     10.0.0.0/24 is subnetted, 1 subnets
O       10.0.0.0 [110/65] via 192.168.64.1, 00:00:17, Serial0/0
                 [110/65] via 192.168.64.5, 00:00:17, Serial0/1
```

1. How many routes does it have to 10.0.0.0 /24?

Two equal-cost routes are in the routing table.

Configure Westasman's S0/1 and SanJose2's S0/0 to accurately reflect the bandwidth of the WAN link:

```
Westasman(config)#interface serial0/1
Westasman(config-if)#bandwidth 768

Westasman(config)#interface serial0/0
Westasman(config-if)#bandwidth 1544
```

After setting the bandwidth, check the routing table on Westasman:

```
Westasman#show ip route

Gateway of last resort is not set

C    192.168.72.0/24 is directly connected, FastEthernet0/0
C    192.168.76.0/24 is directly connected, FastEthernet0/1
     192.168.64.0/30 is subnetted, 2 subnets
C       192.168.64.0 is directly connected, Serial0/0
C       192.168.64.4 is directly connected, Serial0/1
     10.0.0.0/24 is subnetted, 1 subnets
O       10.0.0.0 [110/65] via 192.168.64.1, 00:00:01, Serial0/0
```

2. How many routes are there to 10.0.0.0 /24?

---

3. Which interface is OSPF using to route to 10.0.0.0 /24?

Westasman should have one route to the core FastEthernet network using S0/0. OSPF uses bandwidth to derive cost for each route. With unequal costs, only the preferred lower-cost route is placed in the routing table.

Step 3

Configure a route map to force Westasman to use S0/1 to route traffic from 192.168.72.0 /24 bound for 10.0.0.0 /24. Before you configure the route map, you must create an access list that will match the traffic that needs to be policy-routed. Because you want to affect traffic sourced from 192.168.72.0/24, you will create the following access list on Westasman:

```
Westasman (config)#access-list 1 permit 192.168.72.0 0.0.0.255
```

Next, create the route map, which you will call slow4u. The route map will reference access list 1, which you just created. Use the following commands:

```
Westasman(config)#route-map slow4u permit 10
Westasman(config-route-map)#match ip address 1
Westasman(config-route-map)#set interface serial 0/1
```

This policy will be applied to Westasman's FastEthernet 0/0, because this is the interface that will accept the traffic that is to be policy-routed. On FastEthernet 0/0, enter the following commands:

```
Westasman(config)#interface fastethernet 0/0
Westasman(config-if)#ip policy route-map slow4u
```

Route map slow4u is now applied to FastEthernet 0/0.

After you complete this configuration, use **show ip route** to verify that S0/0 is still the exit interface for Westasman's route to 10.0.0.0 /24.

Step 4

Verify that your policy has taken effect. First, issue the **debug ip policy** command on Westasman's console. Leave this window open.

From Host B, use a trace-route program (such as **tracert**) to trace the route to 10.0.0.1.

During the trace, you should see output from the **debug ip policy** command indicating that packets are being policy-routed:

```
Westasman#debug ip policy

01:02:06: IP: s=192.168.72.2 (FastEthernet0/0), d=1.0.0.10, len
        78, policy match01:02:06: IP: route map slow4u, item 10,
        permit

01:02:06: IP: s=192.168.72.2 (FastEthernet0/0), d=1.0.0.10
        (Serial0/1), len 78, policy routed
```

Examine the output from Host B's trace route.

4. Did this trace hop through 192.168.64.5?

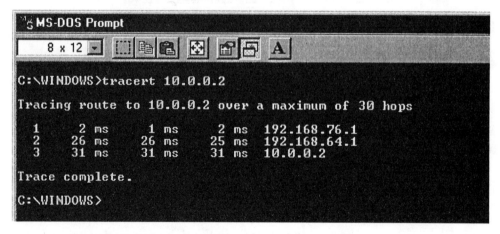

```
MS-DOS Prompt                                                    _ □ ×
Auto        ▼

Microsoft(R) Windows 95
   (C)Copyright Microsoft Corp 1981-1996.

C:\WINDOWS>tracert 10.0.0.1

Tracing route to 10.0.0.1 over a maximum of 30 hops

   1     1 ms     2 ms     2 ms  192.168.72.1
   2    29 ms    28 ms    36 ms  192.168.64.5
   3    35 ms    34 ms    34 ms  10.0.0.1

Trace complete.

C:\WINDOWS>_
```

The next hop should have been 192.168.64.5.

5. Which of Westasman's interfaces did this packet exit from?

The exit interface should have been S0/1.

From Host C, use a trace-route program to trace the route to 10.0.0.2 and examine the output from Host C's trace route.

```
MS-DOS Prompt
8 x 12  ▼

C:\WINDOWS>tracert 10.0.0.2

Tracing route to 10.0.0.2 over a maximum of 30 hops

   1     2 ms     1 ms     2 ms  192.168.76.1
   2    26 ms    26 ms    25 ms  192.168.64.1
   3    31 ms    31 ms    31 ms  10.0.0.2

Trace complete.

C:\WINDOWS>
```

6. Did this trace hop through 192.168.64.1?

7. Which of Westasman's interfaces did this packet exit from?

Host C's ICMP packets took a different route to network 10.0.0.0/24. Host C's IP address was denied by the access list associated with the route map. It was not permitted to be policy-routed.

Finally, issue the **show route-map** command on Westasman:

```
Westasman#show route-map slow4u
route-map slow4u, permit, sequence 10
  Match clauses:
    ip address (access-lists): 1
  Set clauses:
    interface Serial0/1
  Policy routing matches: 33 packets, 4149 bytes
```

8. How many packets have been matches for policy routing?

_____

Lab 7-3: Redistributing RIP and OSPF

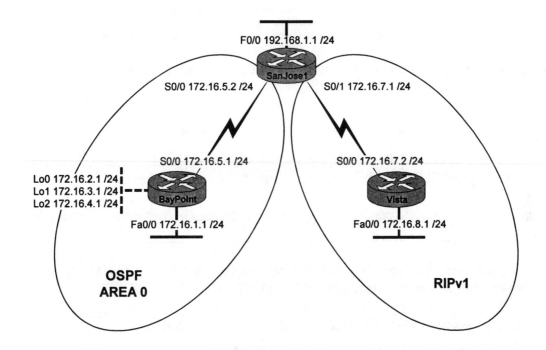

Objective

In this lab, you configure mutual redistribution between RIPv1 and OSPF.

Scenario

International Travel Agency is adding two new sites to the San Jose campus. Baypointe uses OSPF, and Vista supports only RIPv1 until you upgrade hardware. You have been asked to configure mutual redistribution between the two protocols on the ASBR, SanJose1. Routers in the RIPv1 domain should learn about OSPF networks, and routers in the OSPF domain should learn about RIPv1 networks.

Step 1

Build and configure the network according to the diagram. Configure the loopback interfaces with the IP addresses according to the map. The loopbacks will simulate networks within each routing domain. Configure OSPF on Baypointe for all connected networks, and RIPv1 on Vista for all connected networks. Do not configure routing on SanJose1 yet.

Use **show running-config** to verify your work.

Step 2

Configure routing on SanJose1's serial interfaces. Use the following commands to configure SanJose1 routing processes:

```
SanJose1(config)#router rip
SanJose1(config-router)#network 172.16.0.0
SanJose1(config-router)#passive-interface serial0/0
SanJose1(config-router)#passive-interface fastetherent0/0
SanJose1(config-router)#router ospf 1
SanJose1(config-router)#network 172.16.5.0 0.0.0.3 area 0
```

1. Why are the **passive interface** statements applied to Serial0/0 and FastEthernet0/0 in RIP?

_____

_____

There are no other RIP hosts on those networks. Periodic RIP updates should be turned off on all RIP-enabled interfaces that do not require them.

2. Why isn't it necessary to configure any passive interfaces in the OSPF configuration?

_____

Updates are sent and acknowledged between OSPF neighbors. If no OSPF adjacencies are formed on a network, no OSPF updates are sent.

After you configure routing, check SanJose1's routing table:

```
SanJose1#show ip route

Gateway of last resort is not set

     172.16.0.0/16 is variably subnetted, 7 subnets, 3 masks
R       172.16.8.0/24 [120/1] via 172.16.7.2, 00:00:18, Serial0/1
O       172.16.4.1/32 [110/65] via 172.16.5.1, 00:03:20, Serial0/0
C       172.16.5.0/30 is directly connected, Serial0/0
C       172.16.7.0/24 is directly connected, Serial0/1
O       172.16.1.0/24 [110/65] via 172.16.5.1, 00:03:20, Serial0/0
O       172.16.3.1/32 [110/65] via 172.16.5.1, 00:03:20, Serial0/0
O       172.16.2.1/32 [110/65] via 172.16.5.1, 00:03:20, Serial0/0
C    192.168.1.0/24 is directly connected, FastEthernet0/0
```

SanJose1 should learn about Baypointe's connected networks via OSPF and Vista's connected network via RIPv1. Troubleshoot, if necessary.

Now check Baypointe's table:

```
BayPointe#show ip route

Gateway of last resort is not set

        172.16.0.0/16 is variably subnetted, 5 subnets, 2 masks
C          172.16.4.0/24 is directly connected, Loopback2
C          172.16.5.0/30 is directly connected, Serial0/0
C          172.16.1.0/24 is directly connected, FastEthernet0/0
C          172.16.2.0/24 is directly connected, Loopback0
C          172.16.3.0/24 is directly connected, Loopback1
```

No dynamically learned routes should be present. Finally, check Vista's table:

```
Vista#show ip route

Gateway of last resort is not set

        172.16.0.0/24 is subnetted, 2 subnets
C          172.16.8.0 is directly connected, FastEthernet0/0
C          172.16.7.0 is directly connected, Serial0/0
```

3. Has Vista learned about any routes via RIPv1? Why?

_____

_____

Vista is directly connected to all RIPv1 networks, and redistribution has not been configured.

Step 3

Configure redistribution on SanJose1 so that OSPF routes are injected into the RIPv1 process. Use the following commands to configure redistribution on SanJose1:

```
SanJose1(config)#router rip
SanJose1(config-router)#redistribute ospf 1
SanJose1(config-router)#default-metric 2
```

4. What is the default-metric command used for? Do you have to use it?

_____

Check the routing table of Vista in the RIPv1 domain:

```
Vista#show ip route

Gateway of last resort is not set

        172.16.0.0/16 is variably subnetted, 6 subnets, 2 masks
C          172.16.8.0/24 is directly connected, FastEthernet0/0
R          172.16.4.1/32 [120/2] via 172.16.7.1, 00:00:20, Serial0/0
```

```
C        172.16.7.0/24 is directly connected, Serial0/0
R        172.16.1.0/24 [120/2] via 172.16.7.1, 00:00:20, Serial0/0
R        172.16.3.1/32 [120/2] via 172.16.7.1, 00:00:20, Serial0/0
R        172.16.2.1/32 [120/2] via 172.16.7.1, 00:00:20, Serial0/0
```

5. Has Vista learned about any of the networks from the OSPF side?

_____

Creating a seed metric can minimize routing loops or black holes in your network. RIP can't differentiate between internal and external (redistributed) routes. When a network's route is redistributed without a default metric, the network appears to be adjacent to the autonomous system. Elevating the external default metric above any internal routes is a crude but effective way of differentiating between internal and external routes.

6. What is the metric for each of these routes?

_____

The metric should be 2.

Step 4

Configure redistribution on SanJose1 so that RIPv1 routes are injected into the OSPF process. Use the following commands to configure mutual redistribution on SanJose1:

```
SanJose1(config)#router ospf 1
SanJose1(config-router)#redistribute rip
SanJose1(config-router)#default-metric 10
```

Check the routing table of Baypointe in the OSPF domain. Baypointe has not learned about any of the networks from the RIPv1 side.

7. Why hasn't Baypointe learned about any of the networks from the RIPv1 side?

_____

_____

Baypointe should not have any new routes in its routing table. That's because OSPF will not redistribute routes to RIP subnets unless explicitly configured with the subnets keyword. Return to SanJose1 and enter the following configuration:

```
SanJose1(config)#router ospf 1
SanJose1(config-router)#redistribute rip subnets
```

After you enter these commands, check Baypointe's table again:

```
BayPointe#show ip route

Gateway of last resort is not set

     172.16.0.0/16 is variably subnetted, 7 subnets, 2 masks
```

```
O E2    172.16.8.0/24 [110/10] via 172.16.5.2, 00:00:07, Serial0/0
C       172.16.4.0/24 is directly connected, Loopback2
C       172.16.5.0/30 is directly connected, Serial0/0
O E2    172.16.7.0/24 [110/10] via 172.16.5.2, 00:00:07, Serial0/0
C       172.16.1.0/24 is directly connected, FastEthernet0/0
C       172.16.2.0/24 is directly connected, Loopback0
C       172.16.3.0/24 is directly connected, Loopback1
```

8. Has Baypointe learned about the routes from the RIPv1 domain? What is the metric for these routes?

_____

_____

The metric should be 10.

In the routing table, you will see the redistributed routes tagged with the characters "E2."

9. What do these characters mean?

_____

_____

Recall that Type 2 (E2) routes originated outside the OSPF AS and were redistributed into OSPF using Type 5 or Type 7 LSA.

Step 5

Look carefully at Baypointe's table.

10. Is there a route to 192.168.1.0 /24?

_____

11. Does Vista have a route to 192.168.1.0 /24?

_____

12. Why is this route missing from Baypointe's table?

_____

Interface FastEthernet0/0 on SanJose1 is not enabled for either OSPF or RIPv1.

You can complete Baypointe's table by configuring SanJose1 to redistribute connected routes into OSPF:

```
SanJose1(config)#router ospf 1
SanJose1(config-router)#redistribute connected subnets
```

13. What will be the seed metric for redistributed connected routes?

_____

The OSPF default metric was previously set to 10.

Also, configure SanJose1's RIPv1 process to redistribute the connected route:

```
SanJose1(config)#router rip
SanJose1(config-router)#redistribute connected
```

Check the routing tables a final time. Baypointe and SanJose1 should contain all routes.

```
BayPointe#show ip route

Gateway of last resort is not set

     172.16.0.0/16 is variably subnetted, 7 subnets, 2 masks
O E2    172.16.8.0/24 [110/10] via 172.16.5.2, 00:02:00, Serial0/0
C       172.16.4.0/24 is directly connected, Loopback2
C       172.16.5.0/30 is directly connected, Serial0/0
O E2    172.16.7.0/24 [110/20] via 172.16.5.2, 00:01:08, Serial0/0
C       172.16.1.0/24 is directly connected, FastEthernet0/0
C       172.16.2.0/24 is directly connected, Loopback0
C       172.16.3.0/24 is directly connected, Loopback1
O E2 192.168.1.0/24 [110/20] via 172.16.5.2, 00:01:08, Serial0/0


SanJose1#show ip route

Gateway of last resort is not set

     172.16.0.0/16 is variably subnetted, 7 subnets, 3 masks
R       172.16.8.0/24 [120/1] via 172.16.7.2, 00:00:07, Serial0/1
O       172.16.4.1/32 [110/65] via 172.16.5.1, 00:04:06, Serial0/0
C       172.16.5.0/30 is directly connected, Serial0/0
C       172.16.7.0/24 is directly connected, Serial0/1
O       172.16.1.0/24 [110/65] via 172.16.5.1, 00:04:06, Serial0/0
O       172.16.3.1/32 [110/65] via 172.16.5.1, 00:04:06, Serial0/0
O       172.16.2.1/32 [110/65] via 172.16.5.1, 00:04:06, Serial0/0
C    192.168.1.0/24 is directly connected, FastEthernet0/0


Vista#show ip route

Gateway of last resort is not set

     172.16.0.0/16 is variably subnetted, 6 subnets, 2 masks
C       172.16.8.0/24 is directly connected, FastEthernet0/0
R       172.16.4.1/32 [120/2] via 172.16.7.1, 00:00:22, Serial0/0
C       172.16.7.0/24 is directly connected, Serial0/0
R       172.16.1.0/24 [120/2] via 172.16.7.1, 00:00:22, Serial0/0
R       172.16.3.1/32 [120/2] via 172.16.7.1, 00:00:22, Serial0/0
R       172.16.2.1/32 [120/2] via 172.16.7.1, 00:00:22, Serial0/0
R    192.168.1.0/24 [120/1] via 172.16.7.1, 00:00:22, Serial0/0
```

Vista will not have a route to 172.16.5.0/30, because 172.16.0.0 is variably subnetted and RIPv1 does not support VLSM. The /32 networks you see are allowed by the **ip classless** command to support default networks in RIP and IGRP.

Route Optimization Challenge Lab

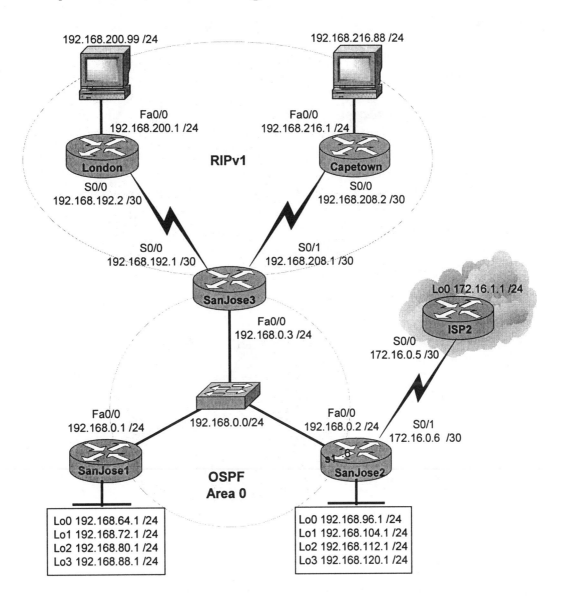

Objective

You create and optimize a network utilizing RIPv2 and OSPF. Your network must connect to the Internet.

Scenario

International Travel Agency is finally connecting its disparate networks. As the network engineer, you are told that all locations need to communicate by the end of the month. The only monies available for the project are for provisioning WAN links.

Design Considerations

You are to work with the existing routers in London and Cape Town that support only RIPv2. For simplicity, you want to propagate a default route from SanJose2 to as many routers as possible. You need to redistribute the connected loopbacks on SanJose1 and SanJose2, simulating sections of your internetwork. Summarize, if appropriate.

Implementation Requirements

- All RIPv2 networks will be redistributed into OSPF. Summarize, if appropriate.
- Use default routes between SanJose2 and ISP2.
- SanJose3 will advertise a default route through the RIPv2 network.
- Redistribute connected loopbacks on SanJose1 and SanJose2. Filter the ISP2 WAN link from being advertised by SanJose2.
- SanJose1 will always be the DR in the core network.
- Minimize the number of routes exchanged between core routers.

Implementation Completion Tests

- Successful pings from all hosts to the Internet (ISP2 Lo0).
- SanJose1 is the DR.

Lab 8-1: Configuring BGP

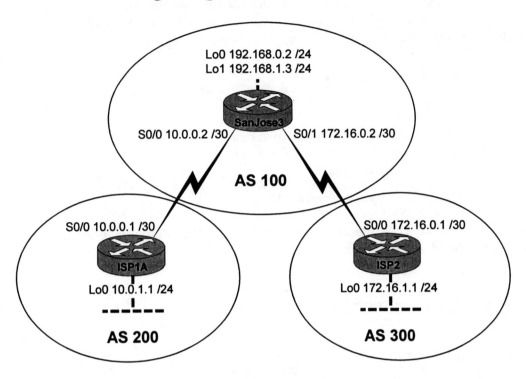

Objective

In this lab, you configure BGP to exchange routing information with the two
Internet service providers (ISPs).

Scenario

The International Travel Agency relies extensively on the Internet for sales. The
company has contracted with two separate service providers for fault-tolerant
Internet connectivity. You must configure BGP to run between the company's
SanJose3 boundary router and the two ISP routers.

Step 1

Build and configure the network according to the diagram, but do not configure a
routing protocol. Configure a loopback interface with an IP address for each ISP
router, as shown. These loopbacks simulate real networks that can be reached
through the ISP. Configure two loopback interfaces with the IP addresses for the
SanJose3 router. These loopbacks simulate the connections between the core
routers.

Use **ping** to test connectivity between the directly connected routers. *Note:* The
ISP1A router will not be able to reach the ISP2 router.

Step 2

Configure the ISP routers. In this lab, you must configure the providers' equipment as well as the International Travel Agency's boundary router, SanJose3. On the ISP1A router, enter the following configuration:

```
ISP1A(config)#router bgp 200
ISP1A(config-router)#neighbor 10.0.0.2 remote-as 100
ISP1A(config-router)#network 10.0.0.0
```

On ISP2's router, configure BGP (as shown here):

```
ISP2(config)#router bgp 300
ISP2(config-router)#neighbor 172.16.0.2 remote-as 100
ISP2(config-router)#network 172.16.0.0
```

With the ISP routers configured, you can now set up the International Travel Agency's boundary router, SanJose3.

Step 3

Configure the SanJose3 router to run BGP with both providers. Use the following configuration:

```
SanJose3(config)#router bgp 100
SanJose3(config-router)#neighbor 10.0.0.1 remote-as 200
SanJose3(config-router)#neighbor 172.16.0.1 remote-as 300
SanJose3(config-router)#network 192.168.0.0
SanJose3(config-router)#network 192.168.1.0
```

This completes the BGP configuration. Check SanJose3's routing table with the **show ip route** command:

```
SanJoe3#show ip route

Gateway of last resort is not set

     172.16.0.0/16 is variably subnetted, 2 subnets, 2 masks
B       172.16.0.0/16 [20/0] via 172.16.0.1, 00:01:24
C       172.16.0.0/30 is directly connected, Serial0
     10.0.0.0/8 is variably subnetted, 2 subnets, 2 masks
B       10.0.0.0/8 [20/0] via 10.0.0.1, 00:01:47
C       10.0.0.0/30 is directly connected, Serial1
C    192.168.0.0/24 is directly connected, Loopback0
C    192.168.1.0/24 is directly connected, Loopback1
```

SanJose3 has routes to the loopback networks at each ISP router. Verify that SanJose3 has connectivity to these networks by pinging each loopback address from SanJose3's console. These pings should be successful.

Step 4

Use **show** commands to verify SanJose3's operation. On SanJose3, issue the **show ip bgp** command:

```
SanJose3#show ip bgp

BGP table version is 5, local router ID is 192.168.1.3
Status codes: s suppressed, d damped, h history, * valid,>best,
        I-internal
Origin codes: i - IGP, e - EGP, ? - incomplete


     Network          Next Hop          Metric LocPrf Weight Path
*>   10.0.0.0         10.0.0.1               0             0 200 i
*>   172.16.0.0       172.16.0.1             0             0 300 i
*>   192.168.0.0      0.0.0.0                0         32768 i
*>   192.168.1.0      0.0.0.0                0         32768 I
```

1. What do the asterisks (*) next to each route indicate?

_____

2. What do the > symbols next to each route indicate?

_____

3. What is the local router ID?

_____

4. Which table version is displayed?

_____

On the ISP1A router, issue the **shutdown** command on Loopback0. Return to SanJose3 and issue the **show ip bgp** command again.

5. Which table version is displayed?

_____

The version number will vary, but the **shutdown** command would have caused a routing update, so the version should be one higher than the last.

Bring the ISP1A router Loopback0 back up by issuing the **no shutdown** command.

On SanJose3, issue the **show ip bgp neighbors** command. Here is a partial sample output:

```
        BGP neighbor is 172.16.0.1,  remote AS 300, external link
        Index 2, Offset 0, Mask 0x4
        BGP version 4, remote router ID 172.16.1.1
        BGP state = Established, table version = 5, up for 00:02:24
        Last read 00:00:24, hold time is 180
```

6. Based on the output of this command, what is the BGP state between this router and ISP2?

_____

7. How long has this connection been up?

_____

Step 5

Check ISP2's routing table with the **show ip route** command. ISP2 should have a route that belongs to ISP1A (10.0.0.0).

If SanJose3 advertises a route belonging to ISP1A, and ISP2 installs that route in its table, ISP2 might then attempt to route transit traffic via the International Travel Agency. You need to configure the SanJose3 router so that it advertises only International Travel Agency networks (192.168.0.0 and 192.168.1.0) to both providers. On the SanJose3 router, configure the following access list:

```
SanJose3(config)#access-list 1 permit 192.168.0.0 0.0.255.255
```

Then apply this access list as a route filter using the **distribute-list** keyword with the BGP **neighbor** statement:

```
SanJose3(config)#router bgp 100
SanJose3(config-router)#neighbor 10.0.0.1 distribute-list 1 out
SanJose3(config-router)#neighbor 172.16.0.1 distribute-list 1 out
```

After you configure the route filter, check ISP2's routing table again. The route to 10.0.0.0 (ISP1) should still be in the table.

Return to SanJose3 and issue the **clear ip bgp *** command. You have to wait until the routers reach the Established state, which might take several seconds.

After the routers reach the Established state, check ISP2's routing table again. The route to 10.0.0.0 (ISP1) should no longer be in the routing table.

The route to 172.16.0.0 (ISP2) should not be in ISP1A's routing table.

Lab 8-2: Configuring IBGP and EBGP Sessions

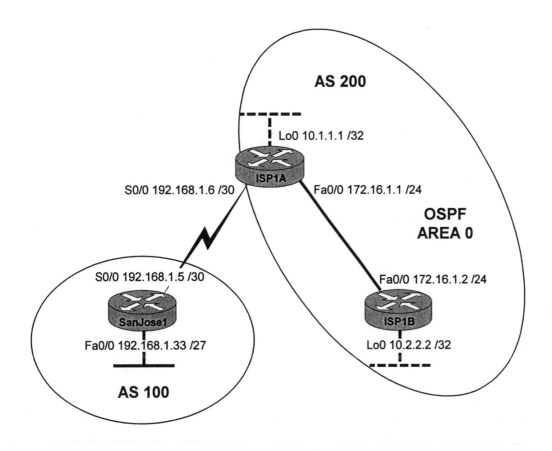

Objective

In this lab, you configure both IBGP and EBGP. In order for IBGP peers to correctly exchange routing information, you must also use the **next-hop-self** and **aggregate-address** commands.

Scenario

The International Travel Agency runs BGP on its SanJose1 router externally with ISP1A (AS 200). ISP1A also runs BGP internally between two of its routers, ISP1A and ISP1B. Your job is to configure both EBGP and IBGP for this internetwork.

Step 1

Build and configure the network according to the diagram, but do not configure a routing protocol. Configure loopback interfaces with the respective IP addresses for the SanJose2 router to simulate locally connected networks. Configure a loopback interface for ISP1A's and ISP1B's routers, as shown. These loopbacks will be used with BGP **neighbor** statements for increased fault tolerance.

Use **ping** to test connectivity between the directly connected routers. *Note:* The SanJose1 router will not be able to reach the ISP1B router.

Step 2

Configure OSPF between the ISP1A and ISP1B routers with the same commands:

```
ISP1A(config)#router ospf 1
ISP1A(config-router)#network 10.0.0.0 0.255.255.255 area 0
ISP1A(config-router)#network 172.16.1.0 0.0.0.255 area 0
```

The **network 10.0.0.0** statement is necessary so that the routers will exchange information about their loopback interfaces. BGP needs this information in order to establish a TCP connection.

Step 3

Configure IBGP between the ISP1A and ISP1B routers. On the ISP1A router, enter the following configuration:

```
ISP1A(config)#router bgp 200
ISP1A(config-router)#no auto-summary
ISP1A(config-router)#neighbor 10.2.2.2 remote-as 200
ISP1A(config-router)#neighbor 10.2.2.2 update-source lo0
```

This topology uses VLSM, so automatic summarization (along classful boundaries) should be disabled with the **no auto-summary** command.

As for the other BGP commands, notice that the neighbor, 10.2.2.2 (ISP1B's loopback address), is not in a *remote* AS at all. Both routers are in the same AS (AS 200). Even so, there is no "local AS" command, so you still use the **remote-as** keyword to specify ISP1B's AS membership.

The **update-source lo0** command instructs the router to use *any* operational interface for TCP connections (as long as Lo0 is up and configured with an IP address). If multiple pathways to the neighbor exist, the router can use any IP interface to speak BGP with that neighbor. This command is typically used in all IBGP configurations. Without this command, BGP routers can use only the closest IP interface to the peer. The ability to use any operational interface provides BGP with robustness in case the link to the closet interface fails.

Because BGP will eventually advertise outside networks that are not part of the OSPF area, you must also enter the following command on the ISP1A router:

```
ISP1A(config)#router bgp 200
ISP1A(config-router)#no synchronization
```

The **no synchronization** command permits BGP to advertise networks without caring whether the IGP (in this case, OSPF) has the route. Usually, a BGP speaker does not advertise a route to an external neighbor unless that route is local or exists in the IGP.

Step 4

Complete the IBGP configuration by entering the following commands on the peer router, ISP1B:

```
ISP1B(config)#router bgp 200
ISP1B(config-router)#no auto-summary
ISP1B(config-router)#no synchronization
ISP1B(config-router)#neighbor 10.1.1.1 remote-as 200
ISP1B(config-router)#neighbor 10.1.1.1 update-source lo0
```

Verify that ISP1A and ISP1B have become BGP neighbors by issuing the **show ip bgp neighbors** command on ISP1B (see the following partial output). If the BGP state is not established, troubleshoot your connection.

1. According to the output of this command, is the link between ISP1B and ISP1A internal or external?

```
ISP1B#show ip bgp neighbors
BGP neighbor is 10.1.1.1,  remote AS 200, internal link
    BGP version 4, remote router ID 10.1.1.1
          BGP state = Established, up for 00:02:18
```

Step 5

Configure ISP1A to run EBGP with SanJose1. Enter the following commands on ISP1A:

```
ISP1A(config)#router bgp 200
ISP1A(config-router)#neighbor 192.168.1.5 remote-as 100
ISP1A(config-router)#network 172.16.1.0 mask 255.255.255.0
```

Because EBGP sessions are almost always established over point-to-point links, there's no reason to use the **update-source** keyword in this configuration. Only one path exists between the peers; if it goes down, alternative paths are not available. *Note:* The **mask** keyword can be applied to tell BGP to advertise a particular subnet when autosummarization is disabled.

Step 6

Finally, configure SanJose1 as an EBGP peer to ISP1A:

```
SanJose1(config)#router bgp 100
SanJose1(config-router)#no auto-summary
SanJose1(config-router)#neighbor 192.168.1.6 remote-as 200
SanJose1(config-router)#network 192.168.1.32 mask 255.255.255.224
```

Use the **show ip bgp neighbors** command to verify that SanJose1 and ISP1A have reached the Established state. Troubleshoot, if necessary.

Step 7

Observe the BGP neighbor negotiation process. On SanJose1, shut down the serial interface connected to ISP1A:

```
SanJose1(config)#interface serial 0/0
SanJose1(config-if)#shutdown
```

After you shut down the interface, issue the **debug ip bgp** command at SanJose1's console:

```
SanJose1#debug ip bgp
```

Bring SanJose1's serial interface back up, and observe the output of the **debug** command (a partial output is shown here):

```
01:09:42: BGP: 192.168.1.6 went from Idle to Active
01:09:42: BGP: 192.168.1.6 open active, delay 17576ms
01:09:59: BGP: 192.168.1.6 open active, local address 10.0.0.2
01:09:59: BGP: 192.168.1.6 went from Active to OpenSent
01:09:59: BGP: 192.168.1.6 sending OPEN, version 4, my as: 100
01:09:59: BGP: 192.168.1.6 send message type 1, length
         (incl. header) 41
01:09:59: BGP: 192.168.1.6 rcv message type 1, length
         (excl. header) 22
01:09:59: BGP: 192.168.1.6 rcv OPEN, version 4
01:09:59: BGP: 192.168.1.6 rcv OPEN w/ OPTION prameter len: 12
01:09:59: BGP: 192.168.1.6 rcvd OPEN w/ optional parameter type 2
         (Capability) len 6
01:09:59: BGP: 192.168.1.6 OPEN has CAPABILITY code: 1, length 4
01:09:59: BGP: 192.168.1.6 OPEN has MP_EXT CAP for afi/safi: 1/1
01:09:59: BGP: 192.168.1.6 rcvd OPEN w/ optional parameter type 2
         (Capability) len 2
01:09:59: BGP: 192.168.1.6 OPEN has CAPABILITY code: 128, length 0
01:09:59: BGP: 192.168.1.6 went from OpenSent to OpenConfirm
01:10:00: BGP: 192.168.1.6 send message type 4, length
         (incl. header) 19
01:10:00: BGP: 192.168.1.6 rcv message type 4, length
         (excl. header) 0
01:10:00: BGP: 192.168.1.6 went from OpenConfirm to Established
01:10:00: BGP: 192.168.1.6 send message type 4, length
         (incl. header) 19
01:10:00: BGP: 192.168.1.6 rcv message type 4, length
         (excl. header) 0
```

2. Based on this output, which state followed Active?

_____

3. Which state followed OpenConfirm?

_____

Turn off debug with the command **undebug all**.

Step 8

Verify that ISP1A can ping SanJose1's FastEthernet address (192.168.1.33). These pings should be successful, but troubleshoot if necessary. Use **show ip route** to check SanJose1's routing table. SanJose1 should have a route to 172.16.0.0. Verify that SanJose1 can ping ISP1A's FastEthernet interface (172.16.1.1). This ping should also be successful.

While still at SanJose1, try pinging ISP1B's FastEthernet 0/0 (172.16.1.2), which is on the same network. This ping should not be successful. Check ISP1B's routing table, as shown here:

```
        172.16.0.0/24 is subnetted, 1 subnets
C          172.16.1.0 is directly connected, FastEthernet0/0
        10.0.0.0/32 is subnetted, 2 subnets
C          10.2.2.2 is directly connected, Loopback0
        10.1.1.1 [110/2] via 172.16.1.1, 00:18:23, FastEthernet0/0
```

4. Can you tell why SanJose1 did not get a ping reply?

_____

ISP1B does not have a route to 192.168.1.0. Because both of SanJose1's interfaces live on subnets within that network, ISP1B cannot respond to SanJose1's ping requests.

Check to see if ISP1B is receiving any route information about 192.168.1.0 via BGP. Issue the command **show ip bgp** at ISP1B's console.

```
ISP1B#show ip bgp
BGP table version is 3, local router ID is 10.2.2.2
Status codes: s suppressed, d damped, h history, * valid, > best,
            i - internal
Origin codes: i - IGP, e - EGP, ? - incomplete

Network             Next Hop        Metric LocPrf Weight Path
*>i172.16.1.0/24    10.1.1.1        0      100    0      i
* i192.168.1.32/27  192.168.1.5     0      100    0      200 i
```

5. A route to 192.168.1.32 exists in ISP1B's BGP table. According to the table, what is the next-hop IP address to 192.168.1.32 /27?

_____

6. Is this IP address directly reachable as a next hop?

_____

Recall that the BGP routers do not increment the next-hop address to their IBGP peers. In order for ISP1B to use ISP1A as the next hop, you must issue additional commands on ISP1A:

```
ISP1A(config)#router bgp 200
ISP1A(config-router)#neighbor 10.2.2.2 next-hop-self
```

After you issue these commands, reset BGP operation on ISP1A by entering the command **clear ip bgp ***.

Wait several seconds and then check ISP1B's BGP table with the **show ip bgp** command.

7. What is the next hop to the 192.168.1.32 /27 network now?

The 192.168.1.32 /27 network should now be in ISP1B's routing table.

8. What is the administrative distance for this route?

ISP1B should not be able to ping SanJose1's FastEthernet 0/0 (192.168.1.33).

Step 9

As a final connectivity test, return to SanJose1 and ping ISP1B's FastEthernet 0/0 (172.16.1.2). This ping should *not* be successful.

9. From what address is this ping sourced?

Check ISP1B's routing table again:

```
        172.16.0.0/24 is subnetted, 1 subnets
C          172.16.1.0 is directly connected, FastEthernet0/0
        10.0.0.0/32 is subnetted, 2 subnets
C          10.2.2.2 is directly connected, Loopback0
O          10.1.1.1 [110/2] via 172.16.1.1, 00:28:38, FastEthernet0/0
        192.168.1.0/27 is subnetted, 1 subnets
B          192.168.1.32 [200/0] via 10.1.1.1, 00:03:27
```

10. Why is this ping still not replied to?

When SanJose1 pings ISP1B, SanJose1 uses its closest IP interface, which, in this case, is 192.168.1.5. Note that the 192.168.1.4 /30 network is not yet in RTC's table, so ISP1B cannot reply to 192.168.1.5. There are several different ways to correct this. One approach is to have ISP1A send a summary address to ISP1B.

For the purposes of this lab, assume that AS 100 includes subnets from both the 192.168.0.0 and 192.168.1.0 address space. You need to configure BGP to propagate a supernet route that will advertise this fact. Configure SanJose1, as shown here:

```
SanJose1(config)#router bgp 100
RTA(config-router)#aggregate-address 192.168.0.0 255.255.254.0
```

After you complete this configuration, check SanJose1's routing table:

```
     172.16.0.0/24 is subnetted, 1 subnets
B        172.16.1.0 [20/0] via 192.168.1.6, 00:07:05
     192.168.1.0/24 is variably subnetted, 2 subnets, 2 masks
C        192.168.1.32/27 is directly connected, FastEthernet0/0
C        192.168.1.4/30 is directly connected, Serial0/1
B    192.168.0.0/23 [200/0] via 0.0.0.0, 00:00:39, Null0
```

11. From where is the route to 192.168.0.0 /23 sourced?

_____

12. What interface is this route mapped to? Explain.

_____

_____

At ISP1A, issue the **clear ip bgp *** command to reset the BGP tables. Wait several seconds, and then check ISP1B's routing table.

13. Does ISP1B receive the summary route?

_____

Verify that the supernet configuration is working. From SanJose1, ping ISP1B's FastEthernet interface, 172.16.1.2. This ping should, at last, be successful.

Lab 8-3: Using the AS_PATH Attribute

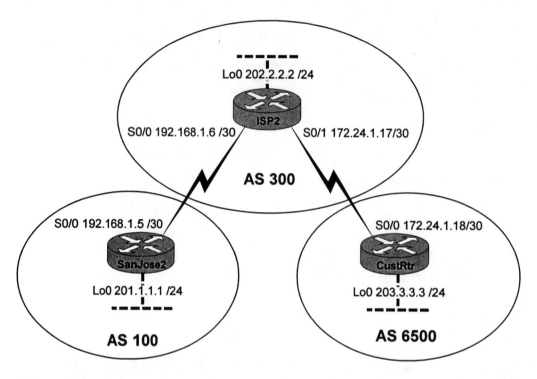

Objective

In this lab, you use BGP commands to prevent private AS numbers from being advertised to the outside world. You also use the AS_PATH attribute to filter BGP routes based on their source AS numbers.

Scenario

The International Travel Agency's Internet service provider ISP2 has been assigned an AS number of 300. This provider uses BGP to exchange routing information with several customer networks. Each customer network is assigned an AS number from the private range, such as AS 65000. Before leaving the provider's network, these private AS numbers must be stripped from the AS_PATH information. You are asked to configure this. In addition, Provider ISP2 would like to prevent its customer networks from receiving route information from International Travel Agency's AS 100. You need to use the AS_PATH attribute to implement this policy.

Step 1

Build and configure the network according to the diagram, but do not configure a routing protocol.

Use **ping** to test connectivity between the directly connected routers.
Note: SanJose2 will not be able to reach ISP2's customer network, CustRtr.

Step 2

Configure BGP for normal operation. Enter the appropriate BGP commands on each router so that they advertise their Ethernet networks:

```
SanJose2(config)#router bgp 100
SanJose2(config-router)#no synchronization
SanJose2(config-router)#neighbor 192.168.1.6 remote-as 300
SanJose2(config-router)#network 201.1.1.0

ISP2(config)#router bgp 300
ISP2(config-router)#no synchronization
ISP2(config-router)#neighbor 192.168.1.5 remote-as 100
ISP2(config-router)#neighbor 172.24.1.18 remote-as 65000
ISP2(config-router)#network 202.2.2.0

CustRtr(config)#router bgp 65000
CustRtr(config-router)#no synchronization
CustRtr(config-router)#neighbor 172.24.1.17 remote-as 300
CustRtr(config-router)#network 203.3.3.0
```

Verify that these routers have established the appropriate neighbor relationships by issuing the **show ip bgp neighbors** command at each router.

Step 3

Check SanJose2's routing table by using the **show ip route** command. SanJose2 should have a route to both 202.2.2.0 and 203.3.3.0. Troubleshoot, if necessary.

Check SanJose2's BGP table by using the **show ip bgp** command. Note the AS path for the 203.3.3.0 network. The AS 65000 should be listed in the path to 203.3.3.0. Why is this a problem?

Configure ISP2 to strip the private AS numbers from BGP routes exchanged with SanJose2. Use the following commands:

```
ISP2(config)#router bgp 300
ISP2(config-router)#neighbor 192.168.1.5 remove-private-as
```

After you issue these commands, use the **clear ip bgp *** command on SanJose2 to reestablish the BGP relationships between the three routers.

Wait several seconds, and then return to SanJose2 to check its routing table.

1. Does SanJose2 still have a route to 203.3.3.0?

_____

SanJose2 should be able to ping 203.3.3.3.

Now check SanJose2's BGP table. The AS_PATH to the 203.3.3.0 network should be AS 300.

Step 4

As a final configuration, you use the AS_PATH attribute to filter routes based on their origin. In a complex environment, this attribute can be used to enforce routing policy. In this case, you must configure Provider ISP2 so that its router (ISP2) does not propagate routes that originate from AS 100 to the customer router (CustRtr).

First, you must configure a special kind of access list to match BGP routes with an AS_PATH attribute that both begins and ends with the number 100. Enter the following commands on ISP2:

```
ISP2(config)#ip as-path access-list 1 deny ^100$
ISP2(config)#ip as-path access-list 1 permit .*
```

The first command uses the ^ character to indicate that the AS_PATH must begin with the given number, 100. The $ character indicates that the AS_PATH attribute must also end with 100. Essentially, this statement matches only paths that are sourced from AS 100. Other paths, which might include AS 100 along the way, will not match this list.

In the second statement, the . character is a wildcard, and the * symbol stands for a repetition of the wildcard. Together, .* matches any value of the AS_PATH attribute, which in effect permits any update that has not been denied by the previous **access-list** statement.

Now that you configured the access list, apply it to the appropriate neighbor (CustRtr):

```
ISP2(config)#router bgp 300
ISP2(config-router)#neighbor 172.24.1.18 filter-list 1 out
```

The **out** keyword specifies that the list should be applied to routing information sent to this neighbor.

Use the **clear ip bgp *** command to reset the routing information. Wait several seconds, and then check ISP2's routing table. The route to 201.1.1.0 should be in the routing table.

Check CustRtr's routing table. It should not have a route to 201.1.1.0 in its routing table.

Return to ISP2 and verify that your filter is working as intended. Issue the command **show ip bgp regexp ^100$**.
The output of this command shows all matches for the regular expression that you used in your access list. The path to 201.1.1.0 matches the access list and is filtered out of updates to CustRtr.

Lab 8-4: Using the LOCAL_PREF and MED Attributes

Fa0/0 200.100.50.1 /24

SanJose3

S0/0 192.168.1.6 /30   S0/1 172.24.1.17 /30

Undesired Link   AS 300   **Desired Link**

S0/0 192.168.1.5 /30   S0/0 172.24.1.18 /30

S0/1 10.1.1.1 /30

ISP1A   ISP1B

S0/1 10.1.1.2 /30

AS 200   AS 400

Objective

In this lab, you use the LOCAL_PREF and MED attributes to modify BGP's behavior and implement routing policy.

Scenario

You are asked by International Travel Agency's Internet service provider to configure BGP routing policies for its autonomous systems. This high-tier provider makes use of two different AS numbers. They asked you to configure BGP so that traffic always uses a designated path to reach networks in International Travel Agency's AS 100.

First, they would like you to configure the LOCAL_PREF attributes on routers ISP1A and ISP1B so that they always use this path to reach AS 100. Second, the ISP wants you to use the MED attribute to influence SanJose3's BGP routing decisions. By configuring the MED, you must force SanJose3 to always use the desired path to reach the 10.0.0.0 network.

Step 1

Build and configure the network according to the diagram, but do not configure a routing protocol.

Use **ping** to test connectivity between the directly connected routers.

Step 2

Configure BGP for normal operation. Enter the appropriate BGP commands so that SanJose3 advertises its Ethernet network and the other routers advertise the 10.0.0.0 network:

```
ISP1A(config)#router bgp 200
ISP1A(config-router)#neighbor 192.168.1.6 remote-as 100
ISP1A(config-router)#neighbor 10.1.1.2 remote-as 400
ISP1A(config-router)#network 10.0.0.0

SanJose3(config)#router bgp 100
SanJose3(config-router)#neighbor 192.168.1.5 remote-as 200
SanJose3(config-router)#neighbor 172.24.1.18 remote-as 400
SanJose3(config-router)#network 200.100.50.0

ISP1B(config)#router bgp 400
ISP1B(config-router)#neighbor 172.24.1.17 remote-as 100
ISP1B(config-router)#neighbor 10.1.1.1 remote-as 200
ISP1B(config-router)#network 10.0.0.0
```

Verify that these routers have established the appropriate neighbor relationships by issuing the **show ip bgp neighbor** command at each router.

Step 3

Check ISP1A's routing table. According to ISP1A's routing table, SanJose3 (192.168.1.6) should be used to reach 200.100.50.0 /24.

Check ISP1A's BGP table. Note that ISP1A has learned about two paths to 200.100.50.0 /24.

1. Which path is better?

_____

At ISP1A's console, issue the command **show ip bgp 200.100.50.0**.

2. Based on the output of this command, what is the local preference value of paths 1 and 2?

_____

Your task is to configure ISP1A to apply a local preference value so that the router will use the other path to 200.100.50.0 (via ISP1B).

Start by configuring a route map on ISP1A that will set the local preference value to 150, which is higher (and thus, better) than 100:

```
ISP1A(config)#route-map viaAS400
ISP1A(config-route-map)#set local-preference 150
ISP1A(config)#router bgp 200
ISP1A(config-router)#neighbor 10.1.1.2 route-map viaAS400 in
```

After you complete this configuration, issue the **clear ip bgp** * command on ISP1A. Wait several seconds, and then use the **show ip bgp** command to view ISP1A's BGP table. Both paths should again be present in the table, but the best path should now be the route via ISP1B (10.1.1.2).

3. According to the output of this command, what is the local preference value of the route to 200.100.50.0 via 10.1.1.2?

_____

Note that no local preference value is displayed for the route via 192.168.1.6, because this route has a default local preference value of 100, and default values are not listed in the BGP table.

Check ISP1A's routing table.

4. Is the route to 200.100.50.0/24 via 10.1.1.2 installed?

_____

Step 4

Finally, you configure ISP1A and ISP1B so that they send different metrics to ISP1B about the network 10.0.0.0. This method allows you to influence the path selection of a router that is not necessarily under your administrative control.

SanJose3 should have two paths to the 10.0.0.0 network. As currently configured, SanJose3 will install the first path it learns about in the routing table as the best path. You will alter the MED values sent to SanJose3 in order to force the router to always choose the path via ISP1B.

First, configure ISP1A to advertise a relatively high metric in updates to ISP1B:

```
ISP1A(config)#route-map badmetric
ISP1A(config-route-map)#set metric 150
ISP1A(config-route-map)#router bgp 200
ISP1A(config-router)#neighbor 192.168.1.6 route-map badmetric out
```

Next, configure ISP1B to advertise a relatively low metric in updates to SanJose3:

```
ISP1B(config)#route-map goodmetric
ISP1B(config-route-map)#set metric 50
ISP1B(config-route-map)#router bgp 400
ISP1B(config-router)#neighbor 172.24.1.17 route-map goodmetric out
```

After you configure these two routers to advertise different metrics to SanJose3, you must also configure SanJose3 so that it compares metrics from different autonomous systems:

```
SanJose3(config)#router bgp 100
SanJose3(config-router)#bgp always-compare-med
```

Issue the **clear ip bgp *** command on SanJose3, wait several seconds, and then check SanJose3's BGP table with the command **show ip bgp**. SanJose3 should have two paths to the 10.0.0.0 network, but each path will have a different metric.

Check SanJose3's BGP table. The best next hop to 10.0.0.0/8 should be 172.24.1.18.

5. What is the metric value of this route to 10.0.0.0/8?

_____

6. What is the default metric value of BGP routes?

_____

Lab 9-1: BGP Route Reflectors and Route Filters

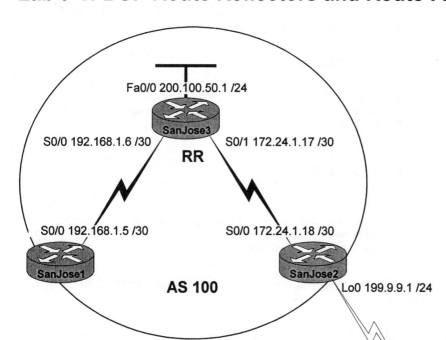

Objective

In this lab, you configure IBGP routers to use a route reflector and a simple route filter.

Scenario

The International Travel Agency maintains an IBGP mesh that has quickly scaled beyond 100 routers. The company wants to implement route reflectors to work around IBGP's full-mesh requirement. You are asked to configure a small cluster and observe how BGP operates in this configuration. You also are asked to use IP prefix filters to control the updates between IBGP peers.

Step 1

Build and configure the network according to the diagram, and use RIP as the IGP. You can ignore the 199.9.9.0 network for now. Use **ping** to test connectivity among all interfaces. Each router should have a complete routing table.

Step 2

Configure the IBGP peers for BGP. SanJose3 will act as the route reflector, so you must configure it to peer with both of the other routers, as shown:

```
SanJose3(config)#router bgp 100
SanJose3(config-router)#neighbor 192.168.1.5 remote-as 100
SanJose3(config-router)#neighbor 172.24.1.18 remote-as 100
SanJose3(config-router)#no auto-summary
SanJose3(config-router)#no synchronization
SanJose3(config-router)#network 200.100.50.0
```

After you configure SanJose3, you can configure the other two routers as route reflector clients. Remember that to set up clients, you merely configure peering between the client and the server; you don't need to configure an IBGP full mesh.

Issue the following commands on SanJose1:

```
SanJose1(config)#router bgp 100
SanJose1(config-router)#neighbor 192.168.1.6 remote-as 100
SanJose1(config-router)#no auto-summary
SanJose1(config-router)#no synchronization
```

Issue the following commands on SanJose2:

```
SanJose2(config)#router bgp 100
SanJose2(config-router)#neighbor 172.24.1.17 remote-as 100
SanJose2(config-router)#no auto-summary
SanJose2(config-router)#no synchronization
```

Verify that SanJose3 has established a peering relationship with both SanJose1 and SanJose2. Troubleshoot, as necessary.

1. SanJose1 and SanJose2 should not have established a connection. Why?

_____

_____

SanJose2 was not configured with the appropriate BGP **neighbor** command. As a route reflector client, SanJose1 will not need to reach an Established state with SanJose2.

Step 3

To observe the full effect of using a route reflector, you must configure SanJose2 to inject external routing information into BGP.

```
SanJose2(config)#int lo0
SanJose2(config-if)#ip address 199.9.9.1 255.255.255.0
SanJose2(config)#router bgp 100
SanJose2(config-router)#network 199.9.9.0
```

This configuration forces SanJose2 to inject the external route 199.9.9.0 into BGP. Check to see if SanJose3 has picked up this route via BGP. Use the **show ip route** command. SanJose3 should have a route to 199.9.9.0.

2. Is the next hop for this route 172.24.1.18?

_____

You should be able to **ping** 199.9.9.1 from SanJose3. If not, troubleshoot.

Now check SanJose1's table. There should not be a route to 199.9.9.0.

3. Why should there not be a route to 199.9.9.0?

_____

_____

Remember that SanJose1 is not configured to peer with SanJose2. To eliminate the need for a full IBGP mesh, you must configure SanJose3 as a route reflector server. Issue the following commands on SanJose3:

```
SanJose3(config)#router bgp 100
SanJose3(config-router)#neighbor 192.168.1.5 route-reflector-client
SanJose3(config-router)#neighbor 172.24.1.18 route-reflector-client
```

Verify that you have successfully created an IBGP cluster. Issue the **show ip protocols** command on SanJose3. The output of this command should indicate that SanJose3 is a route reflector.

4. How many clients does SanJose3 have?

_____

Issue the **show ip protocols** route reflector command on SanJose1. The output of this command does not include information about route reflectors. Remember that SanJose1 is a client and not a route reflector server, so it is unaware of route reflection.

Finally, verify that route reflection is working by checking SanJose1's routing table. SanJose1 should, at last, have a route to 199.9.9.0.

5. Is 172.24.1.18 the IP address of the next hop of this route in SanJose1's table?

_____

6. Note that SanJose1 is not directly connected to the next hop's IP network. Why? (*Hint:* From which router did SanJose1 learn the route?)

_____

_____

Ping 199.9.9.1 from RTA. This ping should be successful.

Note that SanJose1 pings 199.9.9.1 even though the next-hop address is not on a directly connected network.

Step 4

For the purposes of this lab, you need to configure SanJose2 to inject a summary address into BGP, as shown:

```
SanJose2(config)#router bgp 100
SanJose2(config-router)#aggregate-address 199.0.0.0 255.0.0.0
```

BGP should now send the supernet route, 199.0.0.0/8, to SanJose3 with the ATOMIC_AGGREGATE attribute set.

On SanJose3, issue the following command:

```
SanJose3#show ip bgp 199.0.0.0
BGP routing table entry for 199.0.0.0/8, version 6
Paths: (1 available, best #1)
Bestpath transition flag: 0x208
                Advertised to non peer-group peers:
                192.168.1.5
    Local, (aggregated by 100 172.24.1.18), (Received from a RR-client)
      172.24.1.18 from 172.24.1.18 (172.24.1.18)
        Origin IGP, localpref 100, valid, internal, atomic-aggregate, best,
        ref 2
```

7. According to the output of this command, what address aggregated this route?

_____

8. What indicates that route reflection is involved in this process?

_____

9. Is there an indication that the ATOMIC_AGGREGATE attribute has been set?

_____

SanJose3 should, in turn, reflect this route to SanJose1. Check SanJose1's routing and BGP table to be sure. Both the route to 199.9.9.0 and the supernet route (199.0.0.0) should be installed in both SanJose1's routing table and the BGP table.

The International Travel Agency has decided to filter specific routes to the 199.0.0.0/8 address space. You must configure a route filter to prevent SanJose3 from sending the 199.9.9.0/24 route to its other clients (in this case, SanJose1). Issue the following commands on SanJose3:

```
SanJose3(config)#ip prefix-list supernetonly permit 199.0.0.0/8
SanJose3(config)#router bgp 100
SanJose3(config-router)#neighbor 192.168.1.5 prefix-list supernetonly out
```

Return to SanJose1, issue the **clear ip bgp *** command, and verify that the prefix list has done its job by issuing a **show ip bgp** command. Troubleshoot, as necessary.

Unlike before, where routes to 199.9.9.0 and 199.0.0.0 were present, you should now see only one route to 199.0.0.0 in the routing and BGP tables. Troubleshoot as necessary.

Lab 9-2: The BGP COMMUNITIES Attribute

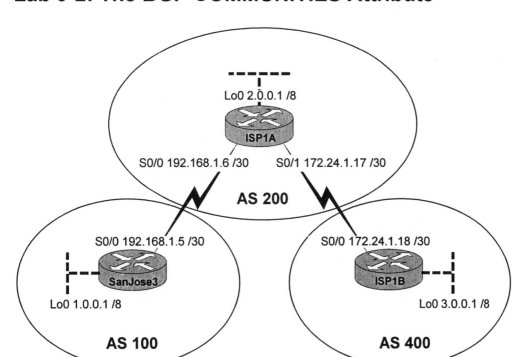

Objective

In this lab, you use the COMMUNITIES attribute to enforce routing policy.

Scenario

The International Travel Agency peers with Internet Service Provider ISP1A and exchanges complete routing information with its AS 200. But, as a matter of policy, the International Travel Agency does not want AS 400 to learn about specific routes within the International Travel Agency's AS 100. You are asked to configure BGP on SanJose3 so that ISP1A will not forward certain routes to ISP1B in AS 300.

Step 1

Build and configure the network according to the diagram, but do not configure a routing protocol yet. Configure a loopback interface with an IP address for each router, as shown. These loopbacks will simulate networks that reside within each AS.

Use **ping** to test connectivity between all directly connected interfaces.

Step 2

Configure the three routers as EBGP peers. SanJose3's configuration is shown here as an example:

```
SanJose3(config)#router bgp 100
SanJose3(config-router)#neighbor 192.168.1.6 remote-as 200
SanJose3(config-router)#network 1.0.0.0
```

When you have configured BGP on the three routers, use **show ip route** and **show ip bgp** to verify that ISP1B has learned about AS 100's network, 1.0.0.0/8.

Step 3

As the International Travel Agency's network administrator, you most likely would not have configuration access to ISP1A AS 200's BGP routers. So, to influence ISP1A's routing decisions, you need to manipulate the BGP COMMUNITIES attribute of the route you are advertising.

Configure SanJose3, as shown:

```
SanJose3(config)#access-list 1 permit 1.0.0.0 0.255.255.255
SanJose3(config)#route-map NO-ONE-NET 10
SanJose3(config-route-map)#match ip address 1
SanJose3(config-route-map)#set community no-export
SanJose3(config-route-map)#route-map NO-ONE-NET 20
SanJose3(config-route-map)#exit
SanJose3(config)#router bgp 100
SanJose3(config-router)#neighbor 192.168.1.6 route-map NO-ONE-NET out
SanJose3(config-router)#neighbor 192.168.1.6 send-community
```

After you enter these commands, issue the **clear ip bgp *** command on ISP1A. Wait a few seconds, and then verify your configuration on ISP1A by entering the following command:

```
ISP1A#show ip bgp 1.0.0.0
```

1. According to the output of this command, what is the community value of this route set to?

_____

Now check ISP1B's table to see if you have prevented ISP1A from updating ISP1B. The route to 1.0.0.0/8 should be missing from its table. Troubleshoot, as necessary.

Lab 9-3: BGP Peer Groups

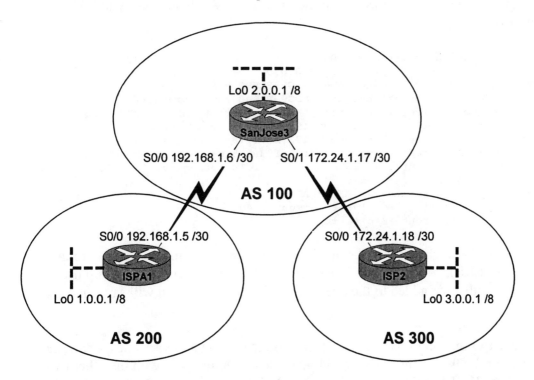

Objective

In this lab, you use BGP peer groups to simplify your configuration tasks.

Scenario

The International Travel Agency peers with ISP1A in AS 200 and ISP2 in AS 300. The company applies similar policies to both neighbors. Rather than configuring policies separately for each neighbor, you decide to configure a BGP peer group.

Step 1

Build and configure the network according to the diagram, but do not configure a routing protocol yet. Configure a loopback interface with an IP address for each ISP router, as shown. These loopbacks will simulate networks that reside within each AS.

Use **ping** to test connectivity between all directly connected interfaces.

Step 2

Configure ISP1A and ISP2 for EBGP. ISP1A's configuration is shown here as an example:

```
ISP1A(config)#router bgp 200
ISP1A(config-router)#neighbor 192.168.1.6 remote-as 100
ISP1A(config-router)#network 1.0.0.0
```

Step 3

Use a peer group to configure SanJose3 so that it will apply policies jointly to both ISP1A and ISP2:

```
SanJose3(config)#router bgp 100
SanJose3(config-router)#network 2.0.0.0
SanJose3(config-router)#neighbor EBGP-PEERS peer-group
SanJose3(config-router)#neighbor EBGP-PEERS send-community
SanJose3(config-router)#neighbor EBGP-PEERS route-map EXTERNAL out
SanJose3(config-router)#neighbor 192.168.1.5 remote-as 200
SanJose3(config-router)#neighbor 172.24.1.18 remote-as 300
SanJose3(config-router)#neighbor 192.168.1.5 peer-group EBGP-PEERS
SanJose3(config-router)#neighbor 172.24.1.18 peer-group EBGP-PEERS
SanJose3(config-router)#exit
SanJose3(config)#route-map EXTERNAL 10
SanJose3(config-route-map)#set community 40
SanJose3(config-route-map)#exit
```

Because SanJose3's neighbors have been assigned a peer group (in this case, a group called EBGP-PEERS), configurations need to be applied only once, to the group itself. The more routers that are added to the peer group, the more time you will save entering configurations.

Issue the **clear ip bgp *** command on SanJose3. After waiting a few seconds, check the routing tables of the three routers. Eventually, SanJose3 should peer with the other two routers, and both ISP1A and ISP2 will receive a BGP route to the 2.0.0.0/8 network from SanJose3.

When ISP1A and ISP2 have the route to 2.0.0.0, verify that SanJose3 is actually applying the same policies to both neighbors. Issue the following command on ISP1A and ISP2:

```
ISP1A#show ip bgp 2.0.0.0
```

1. According to the output of this command, what is the community value for this route on ISP1A?

_____

2. What is the community value on ISP2?

_____

On SanJose3, issue the command **show ip bgp neighbors**.

Check that both neighbors have "member of peer-group EBGP-PEERS" listed as a session parameter. If not, troubleshoot.

BGP Challenge Lab

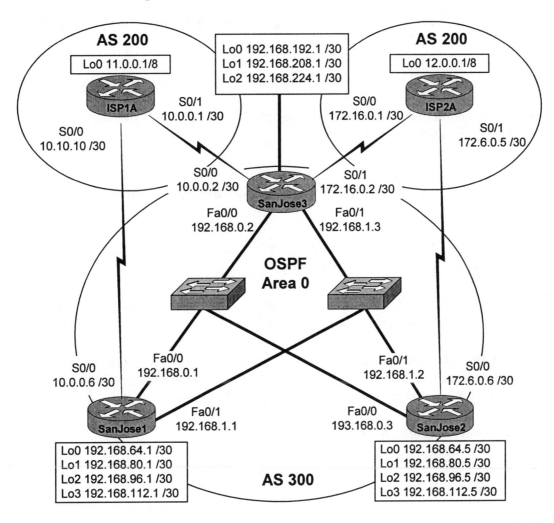

Objective

Configure EBGP between the company's core routers and the two ISP routers, and configure IBGP with peers to create a network that will provide the International Travel Agency with a fully meshed, reliable, and efficient core network.

Scenario

The International Travel Agency relies heavily on the Internet for advertisement, sales, and communication within the company and with their customers throughout the world. They have, therefore, decided to contract with two ISPs. They are connected as shown in the figure. The company requires its network to be readily available and reliable at all times. (The loopback addresses on the ISP1A and ISP2 routers represent other customers. The loopback addresses on the San Jose routers represent networks to regional headquarters and local branch offices.)

Implementation Requirements

- Configure EBGP between the International Travel Agency core routers and ISP1A and ISP2.

- Configure IBGP between the International Travel Agency core routers.

- Only the internal 192.168.0.0 network should be advertised to ISP1A and ISP2 (distributed access lists).

- SanJose1 should be able to communicate with ISP2 through SanJose3, and SanJose2 should be able to communicate with ISP1A through SanJose3 (**next-hop-self**).

- SanJose1 will use ISP1A as its primary ISP through its direct link, and SanJose2 will use ISP2 as its primary ISP.

- If either direct link of SanJose1 or SanJose2 fails for any reason, all traffic should automatically be routed through SanJose3 to either ISP1A or ISP2.

- The International Travel Agency's AS number 100 should be prevented from being advertised beyond the ISP1A and ISP2 routers to the outside world and to their other customer networks (loopback addresses).

Implementation Completion Tests

- A successful ping to every network (interface) from every router.

- The **show** command verifies that routing tables contain the routes specified by the requirements.

Lab 10-1: Lock-and-Key

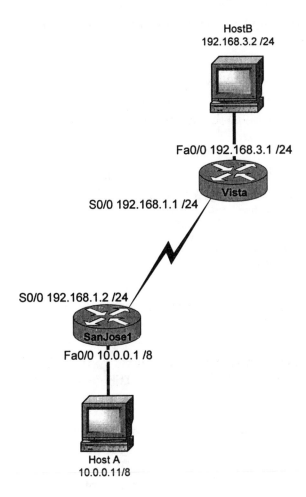

HostB
192.168.3.2 /24

Fa0/0 192.168.3.1 /24

Vista

S0/0 192.168.1.1 /24

S0/0 192.168.1.2 /24

SanJose1
Fa0/0 10.0.0.1 /8

Host A
10.0.0.11/8

Objective

In this lab, you configure a dynamic access list for lock-and-key security.

Scenario

International Travel Agency (ITA) maintains a secure network (10.0.0.0/8) behind SanJose1, which acts as a firewall. You have been transferred to a remote site in the company (192.168.3.0/24) that is not permitted through SanJose1's firewall. The company allows you to modify SanJose1's access list so that you, and you alone, can access the secured resources. Because you work at various stations at the remote site, you decide to configure lock-and-key so that you can get access from any IP address.

Step 1

Build and configure the network according to the diagram; use IGRP as the routing protocol. Be sure to enter the correct network statements.

Use ping and **show ip route** to test connectivity among all interfaces. Each router should have a complete routing table.

Step 2

Configure lock-and-key on SanJose1. You can assume that SanJose1 has a comprehensive access list set on Serial 0/0. But for the purposes of this lab, you need to configure only the portions of the list relevant to lock-and-key.

Because you expect to Telnet to SanJose1 to authenticate, you must permit Telnet access from your remote network. Also, SanJose1 will need to exchange routing updates with Vista, so you must be sure to permit IGRP. Enter the following commands on SanJose1:

```
SanJose1(config)#access-list 101 permit tcp 192.168.3.0 0.0.0.255
    host 192.168.1.2 eq telnet
SanJose1(config)#access-list 101 permit igrp any any
SanJose1(config)#access-list 101 dynamic LETMEIN timeout 90 permit
    ip 192.168.3.0 0.0.0.255 10.0.0.0 0.255.255.255
SanJose1(config)#username ernie password bert
SanJose1(config)#interface serial 0/0
SanJose1(config-if)#ip access-group 101 in
SanJose1(config-if)#line vty 0 4
SanJose1(config-if)#login local
SanJose1(config-if)#autocommand access-enable host timeout 2
```

Note that the dynamic access list statement contains the option **timeout 90**, which places an absolute limit on the amount of time that the temporary hole in the firewall can exist. After 90 minutes, you have to authenticate again, even if you've kept the connection busy with traffic.

The **autocommand** configuration is used to automate the process of creating a temporary access list entry. Upon authentication, SanJose1 executes the **access-enable** command and creates a temporary entry for your individual IP address. The **host** keyword prevents this temporary entry from including other members of your subnet. Finally, the **timeout 2 option** configures the idle timeout to 2 minutes. If your connection is idle for more than two minutes, you have to authenticate again.

Step 3

Verify that the access list is working. From Host B, attempt to ping Host A, which is on the secure network. The ping to 10.0.0.11 should fail. If it doesn't, troubleshoot your access list.

When you have confirmed that the firewall on SanJose1 is preventing you from reaching 10.0.0.11, you can test the lock-and-key configuration.

From Host B, Telnet to SanJose1's Serial 0/0 (192.168.1.2). You are prompted to authenticate with a username and password. Enter the correct login information.

1. If SanJose1 is configured properly, you should be logged out of the Telnet session immediately. Why?

_____

_____

Again, from Host B, repeat your ping to 10.0.0.11. This ping should be successful.

2. If you don't send any more traffic, how much longer will this hole in the firewall exist?

_____

3. Can other nodes on your subnet use this temporary hole? Why or why not?

_____

_____

Issue the **show ip access-lists** command on SanJose1.

4. What indications do you see that lock-and-key has been successfully configured?

_____

_____

Lab 10-2: Reflexive Access Lists

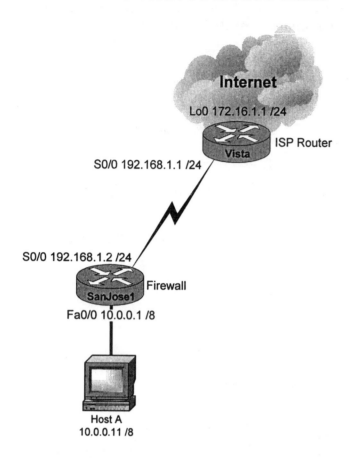

Objective

In this lab, you configure a reflexive access list to implement IP session filtering.

Scenario

International Travel Agency (ITA) wants you to beef up security for its network 10.0.0.0/8. The company would like users on the 10.0.0.0/8 network to be able to establish sessions with remote hosts at will. But at the same time, the company requires that you prevent outside sources from initiating a session. In other words, outside hosts should be able to talk to 10.0.0.0/8 hosts only if the 10.0.0.0/8 hosts started the conversation. You need to use a reflexive access list to implement this requirement.

Step 1

Build and configure the network according to the diagram; do not configure a routing protocol. The loopback interface on Vista will simulate an external network.

Use ping to test connectivity between link partners. Note that Host A should not yet be able to ping Vista's loopback interface.

Step 2

Configure SanJose1 and Vista for static routing. ITA uses static routes to reach the outside world. Issue the following command:

```
SanJose1(config)#ip route 0.0.0.0 0.0.0.0 192.168.1.1
```

On the ISP's router (Vista), you must also configure a static route:

```
Vista(config)#ip route 10.0.0.0 255.0.0.0 192.168.1.2
```

When your static routes are configured, verify that Host A can ping Vista's loopback interface (172.16.1.1/24). Troubleshoot, as necessary.

Step 3

Configure SanJose1 to perform IP session filtering. Configure a reflexive access list, as shown:

```
SanJose1(config)#ip access-list extended FILTER-IN
SanJose1(config-ext-nacl)#permit ip any any reflect GOODGUYS
SanJose1(config-ext-nacl)#exit
SanJose1(config)#ip access-list extended FILTER-OUT
SanJose1(config-ext-nacl)#evaluate GOODGUYS
SanJose1(config-ext-nacl)#exit
SanJose1(config)#int e0
SanJose1(config-if)#ip access-group FILTER-IN in
SanJose1(config-if)#ip access-group FILTER-OUT out
```

These commands create two named access lists, FILTER-IN and FILTER-OUT. The FILTER-IN list monitors traffic coming in via FastEthernet 0/0. The **reflect GOODGUYS** command instructs SanJose1 to create temporary entries in a reflexive access list called GOODGUYS. The reflexive entries are based on the incoming traffic. The FILTER-OUT list will allow traffic to leave the router (and enter the secure network) only if it matches the reflexive list, GOODGUYS.

Step 4

1. At this point, Vista should not be able to ping 10.0.0.11. Why?

_____

_____

From Host A, ping Vista's loopback interface, 172.16.1.1. This ping should be successful.

Lab 10-3: CBACs

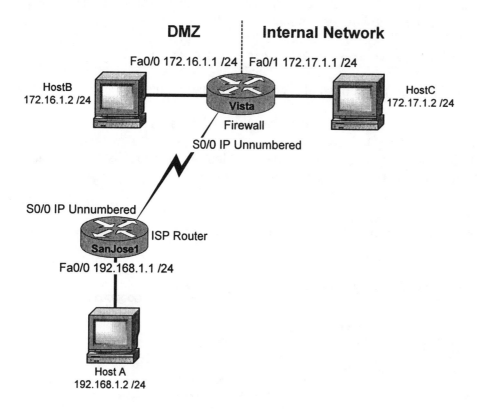

Objective

In this lab, you configure content-based access control (CBAC) to secure an internal network and allow limited outside access to a DMZ.

Scenario

International Travel Agency (ITA) wants you to implement a rock-solid firewall on its border router, Vista. You are to secure its internal segment, 172.17.1.0/24, so that outside host cannot initiate a session with inside hosts. Furthermore, you are to secure the DMZ so that outside hosts can access the public services there, but only if outside hosts initiate the session. To prevent sophisticated attacks, no connections should be allowed to initiate from the DMZ.

Step 1

Build and configure the network according to the diagram; do not configure a routing protocol. Use IP unnumbered on both SanJose1 and Vista so that they use their FastEthernet 0/0 addresses for their serial connections.

Step 2

Configure SanJose1 and Vista for static routing. ITA uses static routes to reach the outside world. Issue the following command on Vista:

```
Vista(config)#ip route 0.0.0.0 0.0.0.0 s0
```

On the ISP's router (SanJose1), you must also configure static routes:

```
SanJose1(config)#ip route 172.16.1.0 255.255.255.0 serial 0/0
SanJose1(config)#ip route 172.17.1.0 255.255.255.0 serial 0/0
```

Use ping to verify that SanJose1 can reach the hosts (172.16.1.2 and 172.17.1.2). Troubleshoot, as necessary.

Step 3

Configure access lists on Vista to protect the internal network. Issue the following commands on Vista:

```
Vista(config)#access-list 101 permit ip 172.17.1.0 0.0.0.255 any
Vista(config)#access-list 101 deny ip any any
Vista(config)#interface fastethernet 0/1
Vista(config-if)#ip access-group 101 in
```

Access list 101 might first appear unnecessary. But in a secure network that uses CBAC, it is important to explicitly specify what traffic an interface should accept. In this case, you expect FastEthernet 0/1 to accept traffic sourced from ITA's internal network (172.17.1.0/24). Although the **deny any any** is implicit, many administrators find it useful to include an explicit entry so that this statement will show up in the running configuration and **show ip access-lists** command output.

Next, you must configure an outbound access list on FastEthernet 0/1. Traffic leaving FastEthernet 0/1 will be traffic originating from either the DMZ or the Internet, so this list must protect your internal network.

Start configuring this list by allowing ICMP traffic, which internal hosts will require to make network management and troubleshooting easier. By permitting ICMP echo replies and other select traffic, you let your internal hosts receive important ICMP error messages from beyond their local network.

```
Vista(config)#access-list 102 permit icmp any any
    administratively-prohibited
Vista(config)#access-list 102 permit icmp any any echo-reply
Vista(config)#access-list 102 permit icmp any any packet-too-big
Vista(config)#access-list 102 permit icmp any any time-exceeded
Vista(config)#access-list 102 permit icmp any any unreachable
Vista(config)#access-list 102 deny ip any any
Vista(config)#interface fastethernet 0/1
Vista(config-if)#ip access-group 102 out
```

Access list 102 effectively blocks all traffic from exiting FastEthernet 0/1 onto the internal network, except for the ICMP messages.

Verify that the access lists have taken effect. From SanJose1, ping Host C. These pings should not be successful.

1. Now ping SanJose1's FastEthernet 0/0 from Host C. These pings should be successful. Why?

_____

_____

Step 4

Configure the DMZ's inbound access list. On Vista, issue the following commands:

```
Vista(config)#access-list 111 permit ip 172.16.1.0 0.0.0.255 any
Vista(config)#access-list 111 deny ip any any
Vista(config)#interface fastethernet 0/0
Vista(config-if)#ip access-group 111 in
```

Again, you have used this simple list to specify the only permissible traffic that can enter Vista on FastEthernet 0/0.

Now configure the outbound access list for FastEthernet 0/0. This list will filter traffic originating from the internal network and the Internet. Assume for this lab that Host B is ITA's public DNS server. Use the following commands to allow hosts to use the server for lookup requests on UDP 53 and to allow DNS zone transfers on TCP 53:

```
Vista(config)#access-list 112 permit udp any host 172.16.1.2 eq
    domain
Vista(config)#access-list 112 permit tcp any host 172.16.1.2 eq 53
```

Next, configure the access list to allow Web, FTP, and SMTP (mail) into the DMZ. Again, for the purposes of this lab, use Host B as the all-purpose server, but you can use the Vista's FastEthernet 0/1 as the Web server, as shown:

```
Vista(config)#access-list 112 permit tcp any host 172.16.1.2 eq ftp
Vista(config)#access-list 112 permit tcp any host 172.16.1.2 eq smtp
Vista(config)#access-list 112 permit tcp any host 172.16.1.1 eq www
```

Of course, the DMZ might also offer services that should be restricted to ITA users, such as POP3 and Telnet. You can accomplish that with the following commands:

```
Vista(config)#access-list 112 permit tcp 172.17.1.0 0.0.0.255 host
    172.16.1.2 eq pop3
Vista(config)#access-list 112 permit tcp 172.17.1.0 0.0.0.255 any eq
    telnet
```

It is safe to allow these services based on source address only if you configure the external interface, Serial 0/0, for antispoofing. You do this in Step 5.

Finally, allow the usual ICMP messages, explicitly deny all other IP protocols, and apply the access list with the following commands:

```
Vista(config)#access-list 112 permit icmp any any administratively-
         prohibited
Vista(config)#access-list 112 permit icmp any any echo-reply
Vista(config)#access-list 112 permit icmp any any packet-too-big
Vista(config)#access-list 112 permit icmp any any time-exceeded
Vista(config)#access-list 112 permit icmp any any unreachable
Vista(config)#access-list 112 deny ip any any
Vista(config)#interface fastethernet 0/0
Vista(config-if)#ip access-group 112 out
```

Verify that the access lists have taken effect. From SanJose1, ping Host B. These pings should not be successful.

2. Now ping SanJose1's FastEthernet 0/0 from Host B. These pings should be successful. Why?

_____

_____

Step 5

After you configure the DMZ and internal access lists, you can now focus on the external interface (Serial 0/0), which represents the greatest security threat. First, configure an access list so that Internet hosts cannot easily spoof your internal network addresses:

```
Vista(config)#access-list 121 deny ip 172.17.1.0 0.0.0.255 any
Vista(config)#access-list 121 deny ip 127.0.0.0 0.255.255.255 any
Vista(config)#access-list 121 deny ip 224.0.0.0 31.255.255.255 any
Vista(config)#access-list 121 permit ip any any
Vista(config)#interface serial 0/0
Vista(config-if)#ip access-group 121 in
```

In addition to antispoofing, this list protects against packets using a loopback (127.0.0.0/8) or multicast address (224.0.0.0/3). Now configure the outbound list for Vista's Serial 0/0. Issue the following commands:

```
Vista(config)#access-list 122 permit icmp any any echo-reply
Vista(config)#access-list 122 permit icmp any any time-exceeded
Vista(config)#access-list 122 deny ip 172.16.1.0 0.0.0.255 any
Vista(config)#access-list 122 permit ip any any
Vista(config)#interface serial 0/0
Vista(config-if)#ip access-group 122 out
```

Access list 122 permits two important ICMP error messages from Internet hosts. It also prevents a DMZ host from leaving Vista via Serial 0/0. CBAC "pokes holes" in this denial entry so that outside users can connect to public services.

Don't be alarmed by the **permit ip any any** statement. If you check your configuration, you will see that both FastEthernet 0/0 and FastEthernet 0/1 are configured to **deny ip any any**, unless CBAC pokes holes in those entries, too.

Step 6

Configure CBAC on Vista:

```
Vista(config)#ip inspect name STANDARD ftp
Vista(config)#ip inspect name STANDARD http
Vista(config)#ip inspect name STANDARD smtp
Vista(config)#ip inspect name STANDARD sqlnet
Vista(config)#ip inspect name STANDARD tcp
Vista(config)#ip inspect name STANDARD tftp
Vista(config)#ip inspect name STANDARD udp
Vista(config)#ip inspect name STANDARD realaudio
Vista(config)#ip inspect dns-timeout 15
Vista(config)#ip inspect udp idle-time 1800
```

These commands create the CBAC inspect list called STANDARD. This list will match sessions for common application protocols. Also, you have to set the DNS timeout to 15 seconds because DNS connections should time out more quickly than other UDP connections. Otherwise, CBAC will have to maintain many useless connection state table entries for long-ago-completed DNS requests.

With the STANDARD list configured, you can apply it to the appropriate interfaces, as shown:

```
Vista(config)#interface fastethernet 0/1
Vista(config-if)#ip inspect STANDARD in
Vista(config)#interface serial 0/0
Vista(config-if)#ip inspect STANDARD in
```

No **ip inspect** command exists on the DMZ interface (FastEthernet 0/0), because outgoing conversations are never initiated from the DMZ. Note that this really means that no outgoing connections are permitted.

Verify your CBAC configuration by issuing the **show ip inspect all** command.

3. According to the output of this command, what is the DNS timeout value set to?

_____

4. What is the inbound inspection rule?

_____

Appendix A

Command Reference

Labs 1

Configuration Commands

Command	Definition
Router(config-if)**ip route-cache**	Enables fast switching on an interface.
Router(config-if)#**no ip route-cache**	Enables process switching on an interface.
Router(config-if)#**bandwidth** *bandwidth*	Specifies the bandwidth for an interface.
Router(config-router)#**variance** *multiplier*	Used with IGRP and EIGRP to configure load balancing.

show Commands

Command	Definition
Router#**show ip cache**	Displays the contents of a fast switching route cache.
Router#**show ip interface**	Displays IP-related statistics and configurations for an interface.

debug Command

Command	Definition
Router#**debug ip packet**	Displays IP packet information, including packets received, generated, and forwarded.

Labs 2

Configuration Commands

Command	Definition
Router(config)# **ip http server**	Enables HTTP services on Cisco IOS.
Router(config)# **service dhcp**	Enables Dynamic Host Configuration Protocol (DHCP) services on Cisco IOS.
Router(config)#**ip dhcp pool** *name*	Enables the DHCP address pool on a Cisco IOS DHCP Server.
Router(config-if)# **ip helper-address** *address*	Allows Cisco IOS to forward a UDP broadcast on a specified interface.
Router(config-dhcp)#**network** *network-number* [*mask* | *prefix-length*]	Specifies a subnet number and mask for DHCP.
Router(config-dhcp)# **ip dhcp excluded-address** *low-address* [*high-address*]	Specifies IP addresses that Cisco IOS DHCP Server should not assign to DHCP clients.

Command	Definition
Router(config-dhcp)# **default-router** *address* [*address2...address8*]	Specifies the default gateway for a DHCP client.
Router(config-dhcp)# **dns-server** *address* [*address2...address8*]	Specifies the DNS server IP address for a DHCP client.
Router(config-dhcp)# **netbios-name-server** *address* [*address2...address8*]	Specifies the WINS server IP address for a DHCP client.
Router(config-dhcp)# **domain-name** *domain*	Specifies the domain name for the DHCP client.
Router(config-dhcp)# **option** *code* [**instance** *number*] {**ascii** *string* | **hex** *string* | **ip** *address*}	Configures DHCP server options for unspecified keywords.

Labs 3

Configuration Commands

Command	Definition
Router(config)# **router eigrp** *autonomous-system*	Enables the EIGRP routing process.
Router(config)# **router igrp** *autonomous-system*	Enables the IGRP routing process.
Router(config-router)# **network** *network-number* [*network-mask*]	Specifies the networks that EIGRP or IGRP is to advertise.
Router(config-router)# **timers basic** *update invalid holddown flush* [*sleeptime*]	Adjusts update timers.
Router(config-router)#**no metric holddown**	Disables new IGRP routing information from being used for a certain period of time.

debug Commands

Command	Definition
Router#**undebug all**	Turns off all enabled debug commands.
Router#**debug ip routing**	Displays changes to the routing table.

clear Command

Command	Definition
Router#**clear ip route** *	Clears dynamically learned routes from the routing table.

Labs 4

Configuration Commands

Command	Definition
Router(config)#**interface lo0**	Specifies a logical interface to be configured.
Router(config)#**router ospf** *process-id*	Enables an OSPF routing process.
Router(config-router)#**network** *address* *wildcard-mask* **area** *area-id*	Specifies the interfaces on which OSPF runs and defines the area ID for those interfaces.
Router(config)#**area** *area-id* **authentication [message-digest]**	Enables authentication for an OSPF area.
Router(config-if)#**ip ospf message-digest-key** *keyid* **md5** *key*	Enables OSPF MD5 authentication.
Router(config-if)#**ip ospf hello-interval** *seconds*	Specifies the interval between hello packets that the router will send out its interfaces.
Router(config-if)#**ip ospf dead-interval** *seconds*	Sets the interval at which hello packets must not be seen before neighbors declare the router down.
Router(config-if)# **ip ospf priority** *number*	Sets the router priority, which helps determine the designated router.

OSPF NBMA Configuration Commands

Command	Definition
Router(config-if)# **encapsulation frame-relay ietf**	Encapsulates the serial interface with OSI layer 2, Frame Relay.
Router(config-if)# **frame-relay map** *protocol protocol-address dlci* **[broadcast]** **[ietf | cisco]**	Specifies the destination IP address that is mapped with a DLCI number.
Router(config-if)# **ip ospf network {broadcast | non-broadcast | {point-to-multipoint [non-broadcast] | point-to-point}}**	Specifies the OSPF network environment to a type other than the default for a given medium.

show Commands

Command	Definition
Router# **show ip ospf**	Displays general information about OSPF routing processes.
Router#**show ip ospf neighbor** [*type number*] [*neighbor-id*] **[detail]**	Displays OSPF neighbor information on a per-interface basis.
Router#**show ip ospf interface** [*type number*]	Displays OSPF-related interface information.
Router#**show ip ospf virtual-links**	Displays OSPF virtual links.

debug Commands

Command	Definition
Router# **debug ip ospf events**	Displays information on OSPF-related events.
Router# **debug ip ospf adjacencies**	Displays information on OSPF neighbor relationships.

Labs 5

Configuration Commands

Command	Definition
Router(config-router)# **area** *area-id* **range** *address mask* [**advertise**	**not-advertise**]	Consolidates and summarizes routes at an area border router.
Router(config)# **ip route** *network-number network-mask* {*IP address*	*interface*} [*distance*] [**name** *name*]	Configures a static route to a specific network.
Router(config-router)# **summary-address** *address mask prefix mask* [**not-advertise**] [**tag** *tag*]	Creates aggregate addresses for OSPF.
Router(config-router)# **default-information originate** [**always**] [**metric** *metric-value*] [**metric-type** *type-value*] [**route-map** *map-name*]	Generates a default external route into an OSPF routing domain.
Router(config-router)# **redistribute** *protocol* [*process-id*] {**level-1**	**level-1-2**	**level-2**} [**metric** *metric-value*][**metric-type** *type-value*] [**match** {**internal**	**external 1**	**external 2**}] [**tag** *tag-value*] [**route-map** *map-tag*] [**weight** *weight*] [**subnets**]	Redistributes routing protocols and connected or static networks from one routing domain into another.
Router(config-router)# **area** *area-id* **stub** [**no-summary**]	Defines an area as a stub area or a totally stubby area.
Router(config-router)# **area** *area-id* **nssa** [**no-redistribution**] [**default-information-originate**]	Defines an area as a not-so-stubby area.
Router(config-router)# **area** *area-id* **virtual-link** *router-id* [**authentication** [**message-digest**	**null**]] [**hello-interval** *seconds*] [**retransmit-interval** *seconds*] [**transmit-delay** *seconds*] [**dead-interval** *seconds*] [[**authentication-key** *key*]	[**message-digest-key** *keyid* **md5** *key*]]	Defines an OSPF virtual link.

Labs 6

Configuration Commands

Command	Definition
Router(config-router)#**eigrp log-neighbor-changes**	Enables the logging of changes in EIGRP neighbor adjacencies.
Router(config-router)# **ip bandwidth-percent eigrp** *as-number percent*	Configures the percentage of bandwidth that may be used by EIGRP on an interface.
Router(config-router)# **no auto-summary**	Disables automatic summarization of subnet routes into network-level routes.
Router(config)#**ip summary-address eigrp** *autonomous-system-number network-address subnet-mask* [*admin-distance*]	Configures a summary aggregate address for a specified interface.

show Commands

Command	Definition
Router#**show ip eigrp interfaces** [*type number*] [*as-number*]	Displays information about interfaces configured for EIGRP.
Router#**show ip eigrp neighbors** [*interface-type* | *autonomous-system-number* | **static**]	Displays the neighbors discovered by EIGRP.
Router#**show ip eigrp topology** [*autonomous-system-number* | [[*ip-address*] *mask*]]	Displays the EIGRP routing table.
Router#**show ip eigrp traffic** [*autonomous-system-number*]	Displays the number of EIGRP packets sent and received.

Labs 7

Configuration Commands

Command	Definition
Router(config-router)#**passive-interface** [**default**] {*type number*}	Disables sending routing updates on an interface.
Router(config)#**route-map** *map-tag* [**permit** | **deny**] [*sequence-number*]	Defines the conditions for redistributing routes from one routing protocol into another, or configures policy routing.
Router(config-route-map)#**match ip address** {*access-list-number* | *access-list-name*} [...*access-list-number* | ...*access-list-name*]	Distributes any routes that have a destination network number address that is permitted by a standard or extended access list, or performs policy routing on packets.
Router(config-route-map)#**set interface** *type number* [...*type number*]	Indicates where to output packets that pass a match clause of route map for policy routing.

Command	Definition
Router(config-if)#**ip policy route-map** *map-tag*	Identifies a route map to use for policy routing on an interface.
Router(config-router)#**redistribute** *protocol* [*process-id*] {**level-1** | **level-1-2** | **level-2**} [**metric** *metric-value*][**metric-type** *type-value*] [**match** {**internal** | **external 1** | **external 2**}] [**tag** *tag-value*] [**route-map** *map-tag*] [**weight** *weight*] [**subnets**]	Redistributes routing protocols and connected or static networks from one routing domain into another.
Router(config-router)#**default-metric** *number*	Sets the default metric values for RIP, OSPF, EIGRP, and IGRP routing protocols.
Router(config-router)#**distribute-list** {*access-list-number* | *access-list-name*} **out** [*interface-name* | *routing-process* | *autonomous-system-number*]	Suppresses networks from being advertised in updates.

show Commands

Command	Definition
Router#**show ip protocols**	Displays the parameters and current state of the active routing protocol process.
Router#**show route-map** [*map-name*]	Displays configured route maps.

Labs 8

Configuration Commands

Command	Definition
Router(config)#**router bgp** *autonomous-system*	Configures the BGP routing process.
Router(config-router)#**network** *network-number* [**mask** *network-mask*]	Specifies the networks to be advertised by the BGP routing process.
Router(config-router)#**neighbor** {*ip-address* | *peer-group-name*} **remote-as** *autonomous-system-number*	Specifies a BGP neighbor.
Router(config-router)# **neighbor** {*ip-address* | *peer-group-name*} **distribute-list** {*access-list-number* | *name/prefix-list-name*} {**in** | **out**}	Distributes BGP neighbor information as specified in an access list.
Router(config-router)#**neighbor** {*ip-address* | *peer-group-name*} **update-source** *interface*	Allows IBGP sessions to use any operational interface for TCP connections.
Router(config-router)#**neighbor** {*ip-address* | *peer-group-name*} **next-hop-self**	Configures the router as the next hop for a BGP-speaking neighbor or peer group.

Command	Definition
Router(config-router)#**neighbor** {*ip-address* | *peer-group-name*} **remove-private-as**	Removes private autonomous system numbers from the AS path from a list of autonomous system numbers that a route passes through to reach a BGP peer.
Router(config-router)#**neighbor** {*ip-address* | *peer-group-name*} **filter-list** *access-list-number* {**in** | **out**}	Sets up a BGP filter for a neighbor.
Router(config-router)#**neighbor** {*ip-address* | *peer-group-name*} **route-map** *route-map-name* {**in** | **out**}	Applies a route map to incoming or outgoing routes.
Router(config-router)# **aggregate-address** *address mask* [**as-set**] [**summary-only**] [**suppress-map** *map-name*] [**advertise-map** *map-name*] [**attribute-map** *map-name*]	Creates an aggregate entry in a BGP table.
Router(config-router)#**ip as-path access-list** *access-list-number* {**permit** | **deny**} *as-regular-expression*	Defines a BGP AS path access list.
Router(config-route-map)#**set local-preference** *value*	Specifies the local preference value for a BGP route.
Router(config-router)#**bgp always-compare-med**	Allows the comparison of the Multi-Exit Discriminator (MED) for paths from neighbors in different autonomous systems.
Router(config-router)#**no auto-summary**	Disables the default behavior of automatic summarization of subnet routes into network-level routes.

show Commands

Command	Definition
Router# **show ip bgp** [*network*] [*network-mask*] [**longer-prefixes**]	Displays the BGP routing table.
Router# **show ip bgp neighbors** [*address*] [**received-routes** | **routes** | **advertised-routes** | {**paths** *regular-expression*} | **dampened-routes**]	Displays information about BGP connections with neighbors.

clear Command

Command	Definition
clear ip bgp {***** | *address* | *peer-group-name*} [**soft** [**in** | **out**]]	Resets a BGP connection.

debug Command

Command	Definition
Router#**debug ip bgp**	Displays BGP state changes.

Labs 9

Configuration Commands

Command	Definition
Router(config-router)#**no synchronization**	Disables the synchronization between BGP and an Interior Gateway Protocol.
Router(config-router)#**neighbor** *ip-address* **route-reflector-client**	Configures the router as a BGP route reflector and specifies a neighbor as its client.
Router(config)#**ip prefix-list** *list-name* [**seq** *seq-value*] **deny** | **permit** *network/len* [**ge** *ge-value*] [**le** *le-value*]	Creates an entry in a prefix list.
Router(config-router)#**neighbor** {*ip-address* | *peer-group-name*}**prefix-list** *prefix-listname* {**in** | **out**}	Distributes BGP neighbor information as specified in a prefix list.
Router(config-router)# **neighbor** *peer-group-name* **peer-group**	Creates a BGP peer group.
Router(config-router)# **neighbor** {*ip-address* | *peer-group-name*} **send-community**	Specifies that a community attribute should be sent to a BGP neighbor.
Router(config-router)# **neighbor** *ip-address* **peer-group** *peer-group-name*	Configures a BGP neighbor to be a member of a peer group.
Router(config-route-map)#**match ip address** {*access-list-number* | *access-list-name*} [...*access-list-number* | ...*access-list-name*]	Performs policy routing on packets that match the specified IP address.
Router(config-route-map)#**set community** {*community-number* [**additive**]} | **none**	Sets the BGP community attribute.

Labs 10

Configuration Commands

Command	Definition
Router(config)#**access-list** *access-list-number* {**permit** | **deny**} {*protocol* | *protocol-keyword*}{*source source-wildcard* | **any**} {*destination destination-wildcard* | **any**}[*protocol-specific options*][**log**]	Creates an extended access list.
Router(config)#**access-list** *access-list-number* {**permit** | **deny**} **udp** {*source source-wildcard* | **any**}[*operator destination-port* | *source-port*]	Creates an access list that filters UDP traffic.

Command	Definition
Router(config)#**access-list** *access-list-number* {**permit** | **deny**} **tcp** {*source source-wildcard* | **any**}[*operator source-port* | *source-port*]{*destination-wildcard* | *any*} [*operator destination-port* | *destination-port*][**established**]	Creates an access list that filters TCP traffic.
Router(config)#**access-list** *access-list-number* **dynamic** *name* [*timeout*] {**permit** | **deny**} {*protocol*} **any** {*destination ip*} {*destination-wildcard*}	Enables a dynamic access list.
Router(config)#**autocommand** *command*	Configures IOS to automatically execute a command when a user connects to a particular line.
Router(config)#**access-enable** [**host**] [**timeout** minutes]	Allows the router to create a temporary access list entry in a dynamic access list.
Router(config-if)#**ip inspect** inspection-name {**in** | **out**}	Applies a set of CBAC inspection rules to an interface.
Router(config-ext-nacl)#**evaluate** *name*	Nests a reflexive access list within a named access list.

show Command

Command	Definition
Router#**show ip inspect all**	Views CBAC configuration and session information.

Notes

Notes